T0158107

FIGHT OF THE PHOENIX

Order of the Delta Dragon

LTC Roy E. Peterson US Army Military Intelligence Retired

authorHOUSE®

AuthorHouse™
1663 Liberty Drive
Bloomington, IN 47403
www.authorhouse.com
Phone: 1-800-839-8640

Published by AuthorHouse 10/29/2012

ISBN: 978-1-4634-1771-0 (e)
ISBN: 978-1-4634-1772-7 (hc)
ISBN: 978-1-4634-1773-4 (sc)

Library of Congress Control Number: 2001012345

TABLE OF CONTENTS

Appendices

DEDICATION

<u>Fight of the Phoenix: Order of the Delta Dragon</u> is dedicated to the Officers and men of Project ICEX and Phoenix/Phung Hoang, which was the program for neutralization of the Viet Cong Infrastructure (VCI), the communist cadre who formed the shadow government in South Vietnam. Army instructors called Phoenix simply, "The attack against and assassination of the Viet Cong Infrastructure." MACV Directive 10-20 was titled, "Organization, Functions and Responsibility for Support to the Attack on the VC Infrastructure (U), Short Title: Phoenix".

PREFACE

Symbolically Phoenix is about rebirth and regeneration. The mythical Phoenix bird burns its own nest, is reduced to ashes, and experiences a glorious rise in beauty and majesty from the flames and resulting debris. Throughout Europe, Asia, and Southeast Asia the symbolism of Phoenix is a powerful vision of enduring redemption and reincarnation.

Begun by the Central Intelligence Agency, Phoenix, as the alter ego of the ICEX program, was extended to the U.S. Army due to the sheer numbers of agents needed in the Vietnam War. Detractors of the Phoenix program focus on what they consider to be the less than humanitarian actions and fail to understand either the symbol or the accomplishment.

Fight of the Phoenix: Order of the Delta Dragon, is all about achievement. My only apology is that I waited 40 years to write my personal account of participation in the Phoenix Program. Phoenix was essential to the victory America achieved in Vietnam despite protests to the contrary either about victory or achievement. Somewhere in the archives is a 1971 (before it was over) study on "Lessons Learned in the Vietnam War". I know. I was a contributor and editor on behalf of the Assistant Chief of Staff for Intelligence (ACSI), General McChristian. If I had access to that product and the opportunity to rewrite portions, I would do so, because my work on the special report was done in 1971, just before my assignment to Phoenix and Vietnam.

Phoenix is a paradigm for all future political engagement, whether military, paramilitary, or civil affairs and certainly pertains to operating in Iraq and Afghanistan in 2011, and to all other countries where direct involvement in nation building is part of the battle. The paradigm needs improvement in terms of authority establishment, chain of command, civil/military coordination, operational imperatives and constraints, and neutralization targeting and decision making, but it is more than rudimentary, it is as lethal as needed.

I checked the Internet with absolute satisfaction that my name has never been associated with the Phoenix Program, not because I do not want to be associated with it, but because my activities remained in the shadows as they should have. I am about to change that, but now it does not matter.

I was privileged to be selected by U.S. Army Military Intelligence to become a Phoenix Advisor in Vietnam. I have read some disparaging works about Vietnam and the Phoenix Program that use the terms "horror, terrible, secret," and the like to describe the program. They are wrong. Phoenix was none of those. I hope this book corrects corrupted thinking by the few that cannot visualize how to win a war with intelligence sources and methods, those who were too timid to cause assassinations of a vicious enemy, and those who sat on the sidelines in the United States and criticized without understanding. May they all join the assassinated VCI in perdition.

PROLOGUE

Flexible Response

1 Corinthians 14:8

"For if the trumpet shall give an uncertain sound, who shall prepare himself to the battle?" (Bible--KJV)

Senator John F, Kennedy campaigning for the Presidency in 1960 found the ideal source to attack Republican defense policy, which was predicated on conventional military attacks and defense structures on one hand and how to handle threats of nuclear cataclysm on the other. A book authored by General Maxwell Taylor, titled "<u>Uncertain Trumpet</u>," set out a new paradigm of communist aggression in third world countries and the need for military operations at the full spectrum of conflict from guerrilla war to nuclear holocaust.

Senator and later President John F. Kennedy who read the book and was briefed by General Taylor adopted the term "flexible response" to describe the defense policy he intended to implement as a counter to the heavy reliance on nuclear deterrence and brinkmanship. Flexible response was intended to beef up the conventional forces and of greater importance, develop and expand unconventional warfare strategies and tactics, doctrinal support, and train Special Forces component units.

U.S. Army John F. Kennedy Special Warfare Center and School

After the assassination of President Kennedy in 1963 and during the Vietnam War, the new military educational institution at Fort

Bragg, North Carolina, designed for development of unconventional warfare and training was named the JFK Special Warfare Center and School. Associated with the JFK Center were the Green Berets, Delta Force, the 82nd Airborne Division, Psychological Operations (PsyOps)/ Psychological Warfare (PsyWar), Civil Affairs, and Project Phoenix. Language training in Vietnamese was integral to the Phoenix program along with unconventional military tactics training, South Vietnam economic and political training, intelligence collection and processing principles, and counterinsurgency methodology.

Selection criteria is rigorous for any program at the JFK Center and is based on past performance of duties, education, existing skill sets such as the capability to learn a language, and psychological evaluation. As I came to understand, I was selected by the U.S. Army Personnel Center and placed in the elite of elite programs, Phoenix. I was an anomaly as one of the only Officers that had not been to Vietnam already and astonished the instructors by being the number one Honor Graduate of the course. I still have the desk set with military insignia awarded to me.

Although I do not remember from my time of training in 1971, Special Operations Forces (SOF) training operates under present (2011) doctrine that is summarized by what are now termed four SOF Truths:

- Humans are more important than Hardware.
- Quality is better than Quantity.
- Special Operations Forces cannot be mass produced.
- Competent Special Operations Forces cannot be created after emergencies occur.

[Source: http://www.soc.mil/USASOC%20Headquarters/SOF%20 Truths.html retrieved January 14, 2011.]

While I subscribe wholeheartedly to the first three "truths", I modify the fourth and add my own fifth "truth" from experience. I modify the fourth point because in Vietnam, the emergency dictated the need. Highly competent Special Operations Forces were developed after the emergency in Vietnam, although a few were in place from initial insertion prior to American direct involvement. The fifth "truth" is native instructors are essential for language training and area orientation, while military personnel previously experienced in the Area of Operations (AO) are essential for strategic direction and tactical training.

Humans Over Hardware

The premise of Humans over Hardware is paramount in operating in an unconventional warfare environment. Only humans can decipher the situation, contact internal friendly elements, and find ways to win the hearts and minds of other humans. Living and working together develops the bond of trust and loyalty. Indoctrinating the indigenous population in the principles of democracy and a free market economy can be performed only by a professional elite that conduct themselves above reproach. Collecting intelligence on the human level often beats collection by National Technical Means (NTM). Having the best available specialized arms, communications devices and hardware; however, does not hurt.

Quality Over Quantity

The Phoenix Program deployed trained professional soldiers and officers within its units and directorates at the JFK Center to teach and train a variety of subjects in the classroom and in field exercises. Military instructors successfully completed at least one combat tour in Vietnam and infused the students with a sense of purpose, duty, survivability, commitment, and confidence. Some of the instructors were scheduled to return to Vietnam the same time as the students in order to maintain operational skills and readiness in their chosen fields and because of the shortened turnarounds of assignments that typically in the Army would have been a three year cycle.

Continuity and stability in the instructor corps was maintained by civilian instructors and staff with field experience and special skill sets to support training, develop doctrine, and publish materials related to the entire range of subjects taught.

I was taught by the elite to be an elite. To say that I did not achieve that status would be to denigrate their efforts and dishonor them. Rigorous selection standards, rigorous training exercises, and intensive classroom presentations insure even the ordinary can become an elite with the proper motivation and training. I owe the instructor corps a debt.

Matching Over Massing

A mass approach to training for an elite program would produce a far inferior human vector. Missing would be the one on one instruction, the hands on training, and the drop in comprehension inherent in such an approach. Matching capabilities and skills, however, takes an already projected leader and shapes those capabilities and skills into a sharpened intellectual and physical human tool.

Existing Over Expanding

Military Intelligence personnel jackets were perused by personnel management experts for language learning potential or in existence for the country of assignment, leadership qualities that had been demonstrated and characterized on annual efficiency reports, commitment to achievement, and character in their professional career and observed behavior. The product of Phoenix education and training produced prepared professionals confident of not only achievement, but mission success.

Native Over New

Native instructors were perhaps most valuable in language training. Co Anh, my Vietnamese born classroom language teacher was married to a Special Forces Officer and insisted on proper pronunciation of the flat tone and the additional five diacritical markings for each vowel of the Vietnamese language for a total of six ways to pronounce one word. Each pronunciation means something totally different.

Brief History of Unconventional Warfare in American Armed Forces

My purpose is not to provide a comprehensive history of American Armed Forces Unconventional Warfare and Special Forces operations. Rather it is to prepare the stage for the Phoenix Program as the next iteration of doctrine and tactics.

Taking a brief look back, American Revolutionary forces fought an unconventional war against the British by firing from behind trees in a guerrilla strategy that confused and befuddled the Redcoats. During the Revolutionary War the tactics of the Swamp Fox, Francis Marion, and his raiders was legendary for the use of unconventional warfare tactics in American history.

Eighty years later "**John Singleton Mosby** (December 6, 1833 – May 30, 1916), nicknamed the "**Gray Ghost**", was a Confederate cavalry battalion commander in the American Civil War. His command, the 43rd Battalion, 1st Virginia Cavalry, known as *Mosby's Rangers* or *Mosby's Raiders*, was a partisan ranger unit noted for its lightning quick raids and its ability to elude Union Army pursuers and disappear, blending in with local farmers and townsmen. The area of northern central Virginia in which Mosby operated with impunity was known during the war and ever since as *Mosby's Confederacy."*

As with more recent Special Forces Operations, Mosby's Rangers not only were a quck strike behind the lines operating force using unconventional tactics, especially speed, maneuverability and surprise, but they were an intelligence collection unit that provided valuable information about enemy troop movements and locations. [Wikipedia article, "John S. Mosby."]

Leap forward another eighty years to World War II during which the Office of Strategic Services (OSS) deployed special operations personnel behind enemy lines, most notably the Jedburgh teams that led and advised French Resistance fighters. The person called the "father" of Special Forces was Colonel Aaron Bank, who was in OSS.

Under Colonel Bank, the Special Forces came into being in 1952 under the U.S. Army Psychological Warfare Division, commanded by Brigadier General Robert A. McClure. The unit was commissioned the 10th Special Forces Group home based at Fort Bragg, North Carolina with the mission of conducting clandestine Human Intelligence (HUMINT) collection and covert actions in a counterinsurgency role. Although the 10th Special Forces deployed to Bad Tolz, Germany in 1953, a training cadre force remained at Fort Bragg as part of the Psychological Operations School and formed the 77th Special Forces Group, which became the 7th Special Forces Group in May of 1960. [Source: "History of the 10th Special Forces Group". *United States Army Special Operations Command.* United States Army. http://www.soc.mil/ SF/history.txt.]

By the time of the Vietnam War, Special Forces unit were already deployed in support of friendly forces on missions labeled Foreign Internal Defense (FID) to work with host nation forces in countering guerrilla activity, provide indirect support, advise local national forces, and collect intelligence. Under most circumstances Special Forces do not engage in direct action themselves in host nations, although the paradigm shifted in the Vietnam War.

Green Berets

Green Berets are the best known of the Special Forces components. They are the stuff of legend and song. The Green Beret worn as a headpiece came from training as commandos with British Commandos in Scotland during World War II. Like their British counterparts those trained in commando tactics were awarded a green beret as a mark of distinction and a badge of courage. They were not authorized as headgear until President John F. Kennedy in 1961 heard about their significance and communicated through channels to the Special Warfare Center, as it was called by then, that all Special Forces personnel were to wear a green beret for his October 12, 1961 visit to Fort Bragg as a special tribute to their distinctive mission.

Recognition and implementation of unconventional warfare strategies could only have been better if it had come earlier than 1960-61. To be sure there were insertions of forces behind enemy lines in the past, especially in World War II, including Maxwell Taylor himself who was inserted, believe it or not, in American military uniform into Rome to coordinate with forces opposed to the Germans and Mussolini. The reason for wearing the military uniform was Eisenhower did not want him shot as a spy if captured. The Green Berets were based on this legacy of wearing military uniforms in an insertion and unconventional warfare role and are associated with Black Operations (Black Ops).

Soviet Proxies

Timing was critical, since the Soviet Union supported, in fact instigated, insurgencies in third world countries seizing on the anti-colonial theme and decorating it with a communist purpose that sounded as a populist call to arms. The Soviet use of unconventional warfare strategy and tactics was to use proxies, as a method to maintain plausible denial of direct or indirect involvement in so-called "wars of national liberation, or self-determination." The Soviets trained leaders in the economic/political rhetoric of Marxism-Leninism, gave them their marching orders, and instructed them to lead insurgencies in third world nations. Soviet support came with the Kalashnikov rifle, Soviet made grenades and rocket launchers, and safe havens.

Soviet support and instigation was no secret. Premier Nikita Khrushchev in January of 1961 announced Soviet support for "wars of national liberation" worldwide. Using words like anti-imperialism and anti-colonialism together with "democratic" struggles was a clever way to assimilate the moral high ground of the west and inflame native populaces. Legitimate governments that took over from colonial countries upon their retreat from power were characterized by communist propaganda as "lackeys of the imperial establishment" and thus were charged by insurgents as illegitimate regardless of how the new leadership came to power. Many of the new leaders had been educated at Oxford, Cambridge, and the Sorbonne. The Soviets sought to remove them through their proxy insurgents much as Stalin had killed the future leadership of the Polish Government in the Katyn Forest Massacre during World War II in an effort to remove western trained intelligentsia from future governmental positions and supplant them with Soviet and therefore communist educated leaders.

No political scientist in the United States recognized the nature of the Soviet strategy and tactics better than Robert Strausz-Hupe, an émigré from Austria and a key figure at the University of Pennsylvania. In his book, "The Protracted Conflict," Robert Strausz-Hupe brilliantly exposed the Soviet designs for world domination and particularly the strategy of using proxies. American academics often poked fun at his writings, but in fact every university student should have been given the text and taught directly from it.

Of course American students were disenchanted with the Vietnam War as were a majority of so-called professors who castigated Robert Strausz-Hupe and anyone else who identified the true problem as the Soviet supported guerrillas and who wrote about ways to win the war in Vietnam and defeat communist insurgencies. Professors, particularly those who teach economics and political science who profess unprincipled views and who support unprincipled activities against American government policies, should be removed from tenure and banished to the hinterlands. During the Vietnam Conflict many of them sided against the United States without an iota of understanding of what was really happening in the world. Professors are often ignorant, even in their own discipline. They in fact were the tinkling bells and uncertain trumpets.

1 Corinthians 16:13
"Be watchful, stand firm in the faith, act like men, be strong!" (ESV)

Professors should be required to read the Bible both for educational purposes and for inspiration. U.S. Army Military Intelligence officers and enlisted certainly receive purpose and direction for courage from such passages of the Bible. I was privileged to serve in such a capacity and took solace from such biblical verses as this one. Central Intelligence Officers that I knew and with whom I worked felt the same way. Together we were ever vigilant, stood firm in our beliefs of God and country, acted like men, and were strong in war. If I were President, I would have all the professors in the country given courses in national intelligence, foreign relations, and American history taught by intelligence officers.

What the American apologists for the communist insurgents never understood was the intensity and magnitude of the killings and acts of terror by the Viet Cong against their own friends, neighbors and relatives. Infiltrating North Vietnamese agents were sent with instructions from the communist leadership in the North and stayed to augment the Viet Cong in South Vietnam territory. The Massacre of Hue by the communists in their so named winter-spring campaign of 1967-1968 is well known and well documented. Eliminating the number of civilians killed in the retaking of the city of Hue and counting only those the remaining population of Hue pointed out in mass graves over the course of a year or still missing, 1,810 were executed by the Viet Cong and 1,946 were still missing and presumed executed by the Viet Cong. [Pike, p. 30-31] Only the number of executions in one place is impressive. The Viet Cong executed tens of thousands over time in South Vietnam, particularly intellectuals, religious leaders, and government officials. That is the short list. A longer list includes families, villages, school children, and informers. Douglas Pike in his monograph for the U.S. Mission Vietnam concluded his presentation on the Hue Massacre and extending it to "what if the communists take over" with the prescient statement, "But little of this would be known abroad. The communists would create a silence. The world would call it peace." [Pike, 42]

American intelligence won the war in Vietnam by 1973. If America had "stood firm in the faith" neither the Viet Cong nor the North Vietnamese would have taken over the south. In the Delta, where I was one of the last Americans serving, the North Vietnamese after being allowed to take over the South without American reintervention in the conflict in 1975, were still fighting anti-communist forces a decade later in 1985. We won! We just did not understand it. We did not stand firm in the faith. William Colby, former director of the CIA and James McCargar published a book titled, "Lost Victory". That sums up the reality of the Vietnam War. We only have the perception of loss and have been stuck with it for four decades, when the truth is we won without declaring victory.

The actual loss of Vietnam to the communist North Vietnamese Army came two years after pulling out American forces under the terms of the agreement in Paris under President Nixon and Secretary of State Henry Kissinger. For all the political acumen, 1973 should have been the date victory was declared by the United States as all military activities were turned over to the South Vietnamese. Kissinger basically forfeited the right to the declaration by the terms of the treaty. South Vietnam then lost to North Vietnam in 1975 as the North invaded the South with tanks and armies and drove to Saigon. American leadership conditioned by the anti-war sentiment in the United States had lost the will to commit forces to stop the invasion, which easily could have ended with airstrikes and incendiary bombings of Hanoi, as I advocated. Where was that Democratic President, Lyndon B. Johnson, when we needed him? Oh, that's right. He resigned over the American political opposition to the war and the methods of running it.

MAP OF VIETNAM WITH PROVINCES AND CAPITALS

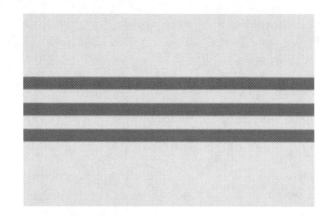

CHAPTER 1

JFK's Own Uncertain Trumpet

North Vietnamese Sponsored Viet Cong Infrastructure Terror Tactics

John F. Kennedy as President blew his own uncertain trumpet on more than one occasion. He allowed the Bay of Pigs invasion of Cuba to flounder and in my estimation and that of a host of observers lost Cuba to communism. He allowed Ngo Dinh Diem, President of Vietnam, to be removed and then Diem was assassinated by Vietnamese military coup as an unintended event. The second uncertain trumpet released untold consequences both for South Vietnam and for the United States. Diem had a lot more status among the Catholics in South Vietnam than any other leader and had kept a lid on a lot of enemy activity and political opponents. Diem was not loved by the Buddhist population, but they hated communism even more and the Catholics lived in a symbiotic relationship with the Buddhists, particularly the Hoa Hao sect centered in An Giang, Sa Dec, and Go Cong Provinces.

What was at Stake

The North Vietnam Communist regime under Ho Chi Minh put in place a shadow government in the South undoubtedly sending agents with the 900,000 that voted with their feet and left the north when they had a window of opportunity in the late 1950's. The National Liberation Front with the alternate name of the Viet Cong mounted not only an insurgency, but a major assassination effort of Government of Vietnam (GVN) officials from the hamlet to the national level and inserted

1

their own cadre. The Viet Cong Infrastructure (VCI) was more than just a government in waiting. The VCI made preparations for North Vietnamese Troops (NVA) for the infiltration of battalion to regiment size units coming in from Laos and Cambodia. The low level commo-liaison links or guides as they were called, would escort the infiltrating units past government observation posts (OP) and around fire bases and move them into prepositioned areas with food and water and in many cases guns and other military equipment. Intelligence was provided on government force locations and potential targets. Vietnamese citizens and especially those in some kind of unit would be forcibly conscripted to be labor, serve in a local militia if showing promise, and placed into main and mobile combat units of the Viet Cong.

Activities mirrored GVN activities including taxation, which was really a form of extortion and bribes that had to be paid in addition to regular GVN taxes thus placing a dual burden, in fact it was more of a triple burden since VC tax collection methods were more heavy handed and the requirements much heavier to bear. VC extortion in fact took up to 70% of rice production from rice farmers who already were not that well off. Terror not only was sanctioned, but the VC were really internal terrorists as we now define the term.

A key facet of VC activity was to compromise those loyal to the government and then use blackmail, extortion, or death as inducements. Hamlet and village chiefs were assassinated, a bomb would blow a bridge on a major highway in the Delta, or an entire school full of children would be slaughtered (I have it in my notes from a daily Tactical Operations Center Briefing in 1972 in Can Tho). The VC was well practiced in covert techniques and in areas north of the Delta had built tunnel networks for hiding by day.

> "By 1967 this network numbered somewhere between 70,000 and 100,000 members throughout South Vietnam. Almost every village had a cell made up of a Communist Party secretary; a finance and supply unit; and information and culture, social welfare, and proselytizing sections to gain recruits from among the civilian population. The members reported up the chain of command, which, in turn, took orders from the Lao Dong Party Central Committee in North Vietnam.

A preferred NLF tactic was to kill carefully selected government officials in order to drive the Saigon regime out of power

"The NLF laid down caches of food and equipment for regular force troops coming from border sanctuaries; it provided guides and intelligence for the North Vietnamese Army; it conscripted personnel to serve in local force (militias) and main force mobile combat units of the NLF, and levied taxes to facilitate the administration of a rudimentary civil government."

"In areas loyal to the Saigon government, protection against the North Vietnamese forces, or even NLF guerrillas, was often compromised because village chiefs were assassinated, bombings took place, or supporters of the government would be executed. During 1969, for example, over 6,000 South Vietnamese people were killed (over 1,200 in selective assassinations) and 15,000 wounded. Among the dead were some 90 village chiefs, and 240 hamlet chiefs and officials."
[http://en.wikipedia.org/wiki/Phoenix_Program]

While the Army of the Republic of Vietnam (ARVN) was fighting a tactical war from home base, behind their lines the VC were undermining the successes as insurgents and traitors. Something had to be done to counter the VC. Enter ICEX with their Counter Terror Teams (CTT) paid for by the CIA and then the evolution into the Phoenix/Phung Hoang Program.

CHAPTER 2

ICEX, 1961 to 1967

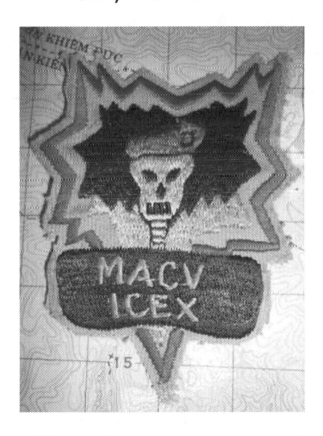

Operation ICEX (Intelligence Coordination and Exploitation, not Infrastructure as some writers have it) was run by the CIA as a pacification program to neutralize the Viet Cong, the "communist civilian" indigenous South Vietnamese infrastructure (labeled VCI) supporting the National Liberation Front as the communists termed it in guerrilla actions and attacks against the government of South Vietnam and anyone, including entire villages supporting the legitimate government. Sources speculate that the program was begun in 1961 with the knowledge and approval of President John F. Kennedy as a method of waging low-level intensity unconventional warfare. There were two components to ICEX and the Phoenix Program into which it morphed: intelligence collection targeted against the VCI and use of intelligence in neutralization of the VCI.

Intelligence collection and coordination is intuitively obvious to the casual observer as exactly what the terms define. Neutralization is not so obvious. Neutralization had a range of actions and programs developed specifically for Vietnam including the voluntary surrender program, resettlement program, and pacification programs, to counter guerrilla actions, capture and interrogation of Viet Cong agents and suspects with incarceration in camps, to assassination.

ICEX never ceased operations, but became attached to the Military Activities Command Vietnam – Special Operations Group (MACV-SOG) in 1966. I used the term morphed into the Phoenix Program, since the military under MACV assumed responsibility for all operations and the ICEX team became more intelligence collection oriented with many if not most of their neutralization targets under the auspices of Phoenix without attribution. ICEX interestingly operated without a disclosed name from 1961 to 1967, when the Phoenix Program was established to functionally replace it.

Statistical accounting for ICEX neutralization of targets is in the range of 11,000 neutralizations of Viet Cong and their supporters and was estimated at 95% of the targets being neutralized with about 600 arrests. [Source: http://www.worthpoint.com/worthopedia/patch-operation-icex-cia-pre-phoenix-100377046]

Enter the Phoenix Program and the escalation of the war in 1967. The Phoenix Program brought a new asset, military intelligence officers, and an infusion of support including psychological warfare for the attack against the VCI.

CHAPTER 3

Phoenix Rising
1968-1972

The selection of the Phoenix bird as the symbol for the replacement and supplementary program for ICEX was masterful by whoever proposed it in the CIA. The Phoenix is a mythical bird of glorious fiery birth and regeneration from the ashes. This sacred firebird mythology ranges from Europe of the Greeks and Romans to Asia of the Russians and Chinese. Certainly Southeast Asians including the Vietnamese new of the significance of the name and the powerful ethos it portrayed. The Southeast Asian version of plumage is blue and green wings and tail feathers, while most of the rest of Europe and Asia envision gold or scarlet plumage and tail feathers.

The central idea of the Phoenix is that it is born from ashes and after a life-cycle of 500 to 1,000 years is reborn from a burning nest likewise reduced to ashes. The first concept is immortality, although in some myths the original phoenix is destroyed and a new one rises. The second concept is the Phoenix punishes the bad and rewards the good.

The Phoenix Program image carried into the Vietnam War for me was one of destruction, annihilation, and assassination of the Viet Cong Infrastructure to allow a revitalized Vietnamese citizenry to emerge. The mission statement was clear, "neutralization of the VCI by any means necessary."

From inception the Phoenix Program was an intelligence operation assigned to CORDS-MACV (Civil Operations and Revolutionary Development, Military Assistance Command Vietnam). Military Intelligence officers were selected in advance for placement in the program and then were recruited by the Military Intelligence Personnel Chief.

The question of how can one wear a military uniform and still be in a special program is understandable. The answer is that if you are one of a few Americans in a sea of American military in another country, you conduct the intelligence operations under the noses of everyone with the understanding that any American is regarded as suspect anyway by the opposition. I learned this later in my military career when I was assigned as an Army Attaché in Moscow. The principle is the opposition knows who you are, but if you can identify the opposition you can still conduct intelligence collection operations under their noses.

I embraced the opportunity to work in a multitasking environment with more than one intelligence organization and enthusiastically accepted the assignment offered me by Major Menohr. I was assigned to the Military Assistance Security Advisor Course (MASA) at the JFK Center for Unconventional Warfare, Fort Bragg, North Carolina in August 1972 with an in-country due date of January 1972 for what turned out to be the last year of the war effort in Vietnam.

Phoenix was not a secret. According to the PHUNG HOANG (Think Phoenix) <u>Advisor Handbook</u>, Phoenix was to be publicized throughout the length and breadth of South Vietnam. The data sources and methods of course were classified to protect the sources and data integrity as any intelligence collection, coordination, and dissemination program and mission must do.

CHAPTER 4

Phoenix/Phung Hoang
Education and Training

Selection Criteria Paradigm

I did not have access to the selection criteria, so I have constructed a paradigm based on my own profile. First and foremost was my Military Intelligence Branch of Army service. The premise of the Phoenix program was founded on intelligence collection, processing, reporting, and direct actions. That meant having completed at a minimum the Military Intelligence Officer Basic Course (MIOBC). Second was having a high score on a synthetic language test designed to ascertain language learning capability. Third was education level, in my case having a Master's Degree and having passed the comprehensive exams for the doctorate. Fourth was having perfect or nearly perfect Efficiency Reports, an evaluation report required to be completed annually by the next level up in the chain of command and endorsed by the supervisor the next level above that one. Fifth was a company grade officer with the rank of 1st Lieutenant or Captain. In my case I was a newly minted Captain.

There was no doubt about it. I enjoyed the intelligence business more than anything I had done in my life to date. Fresh April winds were blowing outside and the air was fresh after a Ft Meade shower. Of course they could not be seen or felt from the inner sanctum of the vault in the large imposing yet muted intelligence building.

"Special letter for Captain Peterson," howled Sergeant Lawson. "It says right here, Department of the Army. Good luck, Sir."

"What do I need good luck for anyway, Sergeant?

"Well sir, you have never been to "nam, have you sir?"

"No, but the Army promised me a three year tour here at Ft Meade and I am only half way through it. Besides they have never called me from MI Branch and I have never called them." That was an off handed reference to the way in which I thought MI Branch normally operated. If you left them alone, they would probably leave you alone, that is unless you had help from your friends and Commander.

Only the week before, Captain Don McKenzie, who was my desk mate across from me and a fellow Dakota born officer had received order to report to Vietnam directly, but he was an artillery officer and had more time at his present assignment. In my thought process the idea did begin to germinate that I might be called serve in Vietnam. After all, I had been deferred for four years for graduate study including working on my doctorate in Political Science.

"I am going to take this letter home and open it in front of my wife." I said. The office seemed to breathe a collective sigh of relief, but of anticipation as well. There was no heckling for the rest of the day.

At home that evening I opened the letter with my wife and young daughter sitting on the couch. "Guess what," I said as I scanned the contents. "I have been assigned to a course at Fort Bragg called the Military Assistance Security Advisor Course and from there I will report to Vietnam this coming January."

My daughter sensed the tension in my wife as she looked at her face. "Don't' worry, honey, I have been assigned to a special operations program called Phoenix."

"What does that mean?" inquired my wife.

"Good question, but it means MI Branch still considers me one of their special officers, or else they would not have placed me in a special program," I responded cheerily. What did I know about Phoenix, other than it was 120 miles from Tucson? Nothing! What did I really know about MI Branch? Nothing.

When I reported to my Colonel the next day, I was taken aback as he said, "Congratulations, I am excited for you. I was afraid you would be the oldest Officer not having been assigned to Vietnam and not having earned some Vietnam medals."

So much for sympathy or direction.

MASA and MATA Courses

The Military Assistance Security Advisor (MASA) course at Fort Bragg was the Phoenix Program, which by 1971 became the Phung Hoang Program with the Vietnamization stage of the war. The promulgation of the Phung Hoang Program by the President of Vietnam did not eliminate the Phoenix program, although the names were simply a use of the Vietnamese language version. According to the Phung Hoang Advisor Handbook, "The U.S. Advisory effort in support of Phung Hoang is called 'PHOENIX'". [Handbook, 3] The five month course included eight weeks of language training, coupled with 12 weeks of classroom instruction, physical training, and field exercises for a total of 20 weeks. The culmination was a Vietnam Village Exercise and the Circle Trigon party representing the communist faction in various proportions in the lifelike mockups of a series of villages with role playing as VCI versus Government of Vietnam (GVN) supporters.

The MASA course was necessitated by the need to teach military officers how to advise on the Phoenix/Phung Hoang program as well as to teach the basics of the program itself. This was not done until 1971, so I was in one of the first course iterations. [See: Ramsey, 41] As it turns out, I was in one of the last as well. The MASA course I attended was designated 2-72, obviously one of two classes taught in 1971, since mine began September 20, 1971.

[Robert D. Ramsey, *Advising Indigenous Forces: American Advisors in Korea, Vietnam, and El Salvador*, Global War on Terrorism Occasional Paper 18, (Fort Leavenworth: Combat Studies Institute Press, 2006), 41.]

MASA was paired with the Military Assistance Training Advisor (MATA) course, the latter of which was designed to provide the combat associated officer positions as the Command Advisors in the Districts and Provinces of Vietnam. That meant when assigned to Vietnam, they would be the writers of the Efficiency Reports of the MASA students assigned to their Districts and Provinces.

There was a missed opportunity to match up the MATA Advisor with a MASA advisor early in the program of both officers and that could have led to an early bonding. I was not assigned until I entered country and was told I would go to the Delta to Military Region IV. I remember that there was a semi-obstacle course that I ran on a regular

11

basis called the MATA Mile that seemed a lot longer than a mile running through the piney woods of North Carolina.

Arms qualification was among the first activities and on September 25, we were all taken to the range to fire the M16. Since this was my first M16, I had some adjustments to make from the old M1 and M14 previously fired. Still I fired Expert with the majority.

Defining the Enemy Target

The target was the VCI. In the introduction to the Phung Hoang Advisor Handbook, General Creighton Abrams, Commander, Military Assistance Command, Vietnam wrote in paragraph 3: "It is emphasized that the advisory effort of all agencies must be directed toward the sustained attack on the VC Infrastructure. The primary operating element for the PHUNG HOANG Program is the National Police; however, it is imperative that all agencies contribute intelligence support and information necessary to ensure the accomplishment of the mission." [Phung Hoang Advisor Handbook: Introduction] The Advisor Handbook defines the VCI well:

"The VCI is the communist shadow government which provides money, recruits, supplies, intelligence and support to VC military units. Its primary mission is to attain effective control of the people and territory of South Vietnam by becoming a viable alternative to the GVN from hamlet to national level. Control of VC military units is vested in the VCI." [Handbook, 2]

Providing money to the VCI came through a shadow "taxation: system for every village, regardless of whether there were any VC cadre who belonged to the village. The VCI taxation system was organized extortion and meant Vietnamese producers down to the farmer with three chickens were forced to make payment to the VCI tax collectors or lose not only their produce and goods, but their lives. Shadow government extortion was in addition to legitimate taxation of the Government of Vietnam in the South and worked extreme hardships on the local populations.

As I learned in the course, there was schizophrenia over the use of the terms Phoenix and Phung Hoang. To clarify one more time before proceeding, the American term for the program was Phoenix. The Vietnamese translation of Phoenix was Phung Hoang. In this context I will use Phoenix when referring to myself and other American advisors and Phung Hoang when using the Vietnamese side of the equation.

Friendships

Phoenix Advisors formed a strong bond, since all 18 of us had been selected for a special program. There were two Majors, twelve Captains, and four 1st Lieutenants. The Majors were going to Provinces, the Captains and 1st Lieutenants to Districts. At least that is what was presented in the course. My primary effort though was not on friendships, but on learning the Vietnamese language for which we had been given tape recorders to listen and to practice and hear ourselves talk. Every evening after eating in the mess hall, I would work hard on the language as I felt that could be my future salvation if captured or lost in the jungle. Language for me was a weapon and defense mechanism.

The friends I knew the best were Vic Gunderson, Raul Chandler, Richard Montgomery, Dick Rice, Bob Rogalski, and Preston Funkhouser. My mentor, however, was Major Coniglio, a very even and well spoken person who I consulted whenever I had a question about Vietnam and Phoenix operations, since he had been there more than once and had a more objective approach to the subject than my fun loving friends.

The group that liked to eat out at least once a week, however, was a different collection of friends. This group usually included Captain Ireland, Captain Berry, 1st Lieutenant Pulvere, and sometimes one of my other friends. One of the first nights at the course we decided to go to a Vietnamese restaurant so my friends could introduce me to Vietnamese cuisine. The restaurant was not crowded and was lit by candles that seemed to be burning incense from the smell. The fetching waitresses in their traditional Vietnamese dresses called "Ao Dai" in this case wearing burgundy ones, touched our backs with one hand as they served. I looked at the dishes set above the plates at what looked to be an oily substance with little cut up red peppers.

Captain Berry was watching me and wanted to be the first to tell me about "Nuoc Mam" and "Ah". "Nuoc Mam" (pronounced Nuc Mom) is a fish oil that comes from a barrel of fermented fish that have been allowed to rot. Over time, and don't ask me how much time, the pure oil rises to the top of the barrel. In Vietnam they grade the oil according to the different levels until they get to the rotting carcasses. The oil at the top is number 1 and at the bottom is number 10. The Vietnamese use this same grade system to talk about people as being either a good guy at number 1 or a bad guy at number 10. The red thing in the oil is a small round red pepper grown in Vietnam called Ah." I could not help myself from asking, "Is that because that is all they can say when they eat it?" Captain Berry matter of factly replied, "Probably, since it is hotter than a habanero chili pepper."

The first dish served was Banh Canh Cua, which was crab soup and noodles. With soy sauce it was very tasty, much like a Chinese noodle soup. Next came spring rolls, which are similar to Chinese egg rolls and everyone began dipping them into the nuoc mam. I followed suit and was rewarded with a very pleasant and hot tasting appetizer with more flavor than the typical Chinese egg roll. The main dishes were all ordered by Captain Berry, one per person, but with plenty for all to share from each dish set in the center of the table. The chicken, beef, pork, and shrimp dishes all seemed very similar to Chinese ones, but with an improved taste. I learned that is because the South Vietnamese use more natural herbs and spices than either their Northern cousins or the Chinese. Mushrooms and shallots or at least leeks were included in every meat dish.

"If this is regular Vietnamese food, I love it," I exclaimed. My friends all agreed that this was typical in a Saigon restaurant, but you never knew what they were going to serve somewhere else, especially in a district. I was then entertained by everything from goat face soup to pig brain dishes.

Captain Ireland explained to me that the Delta of Vietnam had the best food and that the best nuoc mam came from Phu Quoc, an island off the southern tip of the Ca Mau peninsula. I filed that away for future reference.

CHAPTER 5

PHUNG HOANG

ADVISOR HANDBOOK

The <u>PHUNG HOANG Advisor Handbook</u> provides the outline and source material for this chapter. I will amplify the course material with my own interpretations and comments. There are no numbers for the chapters of the <u>Handbook,</u> so I have added them to assist the reader.

1. Government of Vietnam: The Client State

Constitutional Authority and Program
Promulgation [Handbook, page 3]

Client State is a term that I have found used generally throughout the literature of political science and often has a negative connotation associated with communism. Client state, however, is a useful way to describe Vietnam and relationship to the Phoenix Program. The Government of Vietnam (GVN) was the legitimate government of South Vietnam and was the client state for Phoenix operators and later advisors. The section of the Handbook related to the client state is titled "Background."

The authority for the Phoenix advisory effort and the Phung Hoang Program was Article 4 of the GVN Constitution, which was promulgated in 1967 and the follow on Presidential Decree No. 280-a/TT/SL which promulgated the Phung Hoang Program in the image of the American Phoenix concept. Article 4 of the Constitution of the Republic of Vietnam stated:

a. The Republic of Vietnam opposes communism in any form.

b. Any activity designed to publicize or carry out Communism is prohibited.

The Decree of 1968 was thus legitimized by the Constitution and provided the legal basis for institutionalization of the Phung Hoang Program as the law of the land. The statement of promulgation was very concise: "The intent and aim of the (PHUNG HOANG) Program is to utilize existing civilian and military agencies (police, paramilitary, and military forces) in a systematic and coordinated effort to destroy the Viet Cong Infrastructure throughout Vietnam." [Handbook, 3]

So far then, I have learned that the Phoenix program is the attack on the Viet Cong Infrastructure and my objective is to destroy it. I love this program already.

I next learned the GVN "chose" the word Phung Hoang to identify the program because "In Chinese and Vietnamese mythology the Phung Hoang is a good omen of marital happiness, peace, and good fortune." Choice is an interesting idea for speculation. Could it be the simple translation of Phoenix? No doubt. [Handbook, 3]

The methodology for attacking the VCI under the aegis of the Phung Hoang Program is presented as an intelligence collection mission providing targeting data (only implied by the word "collated," but later substantiated in the course) to armed police and military forces:

> "The PHUNG HOANG Program coordinates GVN agencies in the attack on the VCI by placing VCI-intelligence gathered by all agencies in one location, systematically collating anti-VCI operations (often joint enter-agency efforts) based on the PHUNG HOANG Center's data bank. PHUNG HOANG is not a separate agency, organization, or entity..PHUNG HOANG Centers are entirely dependent on the PHUNG HOANG Program member agencies: National Police, RF/PF (Regional Forces/Popular Forces), Rural Development Cadre, ARVN (Army of the Republic of Vietnam), Chieu Hoi (VC that turn themselves in to the GVN, NPFF (National Police Field Force), VIS (Vietnam Information Service), etc." [Handbook, 3]

Although intelligence officers were assigned to Phoenix, their role was listed as advisory only and not even as intelligence collectors and disseminators. According to the Handbook,

> "PHOENIX is NOT an intelligence unit or collection capability. PHOENIX personnel and staff are presently members of MACCORDS at every echelon under the direct command of the senior MACV/CORDS officer at each echelon." [Handbook, 3]

Obviously this is "Vietnamization" at its most poignant. The files to be maintained are not American, although American advisors had access to the files. The South Vietnamese at some point prior to my arrival took over the targeting folders, dossiers, incoming information and disseminated the intelligence to appropriate officials and levels within the GVN hierarchy. Phoenix advisors were no longer responsible for what happened, only for prodding, guiding, and directing counterparts to do their jobs and dragging them along on inspections to the Provinces and Districts to get them out into the field.

Organization of PHUNG HOANG [Handbook, 4]

The Handbook explains that all PHUNG HOANG activities are controlled and monitored by Committees at 1.) National, 2.) Regional, and 3.) Province levels. The Regions corresponded to the MAC/CORDS Subdivision into four regional corps from north to south in South Vietnam labeled MR1-MR4. Districts appear to have been left off the list of coordination; however, in practical effect this was not the case because in the same organizational structure, Province Intelligence and Operations Coordinating Centers (PIOCCs) and District Intelligence and Operations Coordinating Centers (DIOCCs) were established adding the district as the fourth level for coordinated activity. Heuristically districts were left off the committee list because the number of agencies at that level was highly limited. The list of members on the PHUNG HOANG Committees at the first three levels is as follows:

- National Police
- Special Police
- National Police Field Force (Rather like a western posse)
- G2 (Military Intelligence Shop)
- G3 (Military Operations Shop)
- Military Security Service
- Chieu Hoi Service
- Vietnamese Information Service
- Provincial Reconnaissance Unit (PRU)
- Rural Development Cadre (Agrarian reformers and the like)

Intelligence was to be shared among all these agencies, dossiers and target folders prepared, VCI targets selected for "neutralization", and direct action taken. Phoenix advisors were assigned at all levels down to district.

2. Documents and Materials [Handbook, 5]

Besides the Presidential Decree of 1968, the Minister of the Interior was given the task of issuing Standard Operating Procedures for the program in his duties as the Chairman of the Central PHUNGHOANG

Committee. Here is the breakdown of the SOPs plus the "GVN/US agreed upon listing of Viet Cong positions which are considered to be of the VCI cadre":

SOP No. 1: Organization
SOP No. 2: Tools and Working Procedures especially of the DIOCCs
SOP No. 3: Operational Responsibilities at each level
<u>Green Book</u>: Current breakout of Executive and Significant VCI Cadre

Periodic publications included biweekly, monthly, and annual reports and readouts from the Combined Documents Exploitation Center (CDEC lists of names of VCI) and Combined Intelligence Center, Vietnam (CICV). MAC/CORDS Directives and Vietnamese Directives for implementation and procedures including the SOPs were list last. [Handbook, 6-7]

3. Operational Procedures [<u>Handbook</u>, 9]
 <u>SOP No. 3</u>: pgs 66-120

The Organizational Procedures from SOP 3 were reduced to about a half page again stating "The mission of the Intelligence and Operations Coordinating Center is to neutralize the Viet Cong Infrastructure." Furthermore, "An IOCC is not functioning efficiently unless it regularly and successfully targets specific VCI cadres and organizations for neutralization." The steps within the IOCC are further delineated:

* Identification of a VCI with name and position
* Two index cards are prepared, one alphabetical and one for the village/hamlet files
* Prepare VCI Target Folder (name/position/habits/contacts/schedule/modus operandi) I would have added to this list family and photos if available.
* Evidence of VCI involvement sufficient to sentence him/her by Province Security Committee
* Case control with number and importance
* Fill intelligence gaps and levy intelligence requirements to fill the gaps

- Coordinate other files such as source control records, VCI organization chart on which the person fits, Photographic correlation of files, Files on Guides associated with suspect
- Work to neutralize entire VCI staff elements surrounding suspect

I asked the Major from the 525 MI Group what he thought was the best way to neutralize the VC. He responded, "I like the strychnine in the peanut butter trick best." He sounded serious so I did not ask him anymore questions for the rest of the course.

4. Target Data and Dossiers [Handbook, 10]

The section starts with calling attention to the importance of "professional preparation of VCI Target Folders containing both the 'VCI Target Personality Data Form' and the 'Offender Dossier' for each and every member of the VCI throughout the country…" as the "foundation from which successful operations can be run and sentencing be assured by Province Security Committees." Constant review and updating are important with "full use" of the "Information Requirement Form" and all procedures listed in Annex 14 of SOP3. Documentation includes:

- Source reports
- Captured documents
- Interrogation Reports
- Hoi Chanh debriefing reports
- All relevant documents of any type and extracts from other documents

Appropriate postings then must be made both to the Target Folder and the "VCI Target Personality Data Form".

5. Counterpart Relationships [Handbook, 11]

I can summarize this section by the words, make your counterpart your friend, but be firm in advising him. Usually terms for a relationship to be built include trust, mutual respect, and understanding.

Phoenix instructors had a lot to say about counterparts and how to react to them. One of the first items was something of a culture shock. According to our instructors, your counterpart always wants to hold your hand while walking in public as a demonstration of close friendship. Too close, I thought, but whatever. The next concept was even more ominous, eat at least some of whatever they give you and do not ask what it is until you have completed the meal. I could hardly wait for the third instruction, do not attack the big snake. Pythons are often kept in homes as a pet and to eat the big rats. Many counterparts have pythons protecting their families. The fifth instruction went for all restaurants and counterparts as well, do not eat the ice because of the likelihood of contracting hepatitis. By this time I was absorbed with learning everything I could about the environment in Vietnam and working with a counterpart.

6. American Advisory Relationships [Handbook, 12]

A summary of this section is that PHUNG HOANG and the PIOCCs/DIOCCs are the "spearhead of pacification" and all pacification advisory personnel are "responsible for close coordination and cooperation." Obviously this is where the MASA's mix with the MATA's and both deal with any other American advisory personnel such as advisors to the National Police.

7. Advisor Legal Position and Responsibilities [Handbook, 13]

The position and responsibilities of the advisor are absolutely limited by legal requirements. This is the clause that is missed by critics who insist Phoenix operated outside any legal structure, pattern, or comity. The Military Regions in fact had one of the Phoenix team members assigned the duty of Legal Advisor and in the case of MR IV, upon my arrival I was designated the Legal Advisor for the Delta.

Here are the key legal parameters:

- International law
- Laws of the Republic of South Vietnam
- US Military Law and Regulations

The <u>Handbook</u> goes on to state (PHUNG HOANG Advisors) "advice and assistance must be within the confines of this legal framework…." and emphasizes "Participation in actions contrary to law are expressly prohibited." Violations are to be reported and a full report must be made to the "immediate superior for corrective action."

Legal parameters are well defined, reporting of illegal activities are a duty, and there is no room for misinterpretation. Now tell me the Phoenix Advisor did not have limits and could participate in torture or illegal killings. Apparently some researchers that charge otherwise are ignorant of the legal prohibitions of the program.

8. Arrests and Apprehensions [<u>Handbook</u>, 13]

The Phoenix Program clearly envisioned arrests and apprehensions as in any policing activity as the primary method of neutralization. As in any police program, some suspects just do not surrender willingly and are killed trying to fight their way out of capture.

Arrest and apprehension procedures were codified to insure timely proper processing, due process of the legal apparatus, and legal niceties including warrants being issued either prior to the apprehension and arrest or ex post facto. Ex post facto warrants were necessitated by the nature of the crimes being committed and the nature of the VCI.

A VCI suspect accused of an offense against the National Security of the GVN could be "taken into custody and held up to twenty-four hours for questioning and investigation by the apprehending agency." After twenty-four hours the suspect had to be turned over to the National Police. Arrest warrants could be made "pursuant to a warrant issued by a competent judicial authority defined as Province Chiefs, Mayors, District Chiefs and Police Chiefs." For the record and for this teaching point, "US personnel are not authorized to arrest GVN citizens." The arrest order (warrant) was to be issued by one of the following:

- Judicial police
- Militry police
- Military Security Service
- National Police (including NPFF)
- Citizen's arrest: Any person who witnessed the commission of a crime "in flagrante delicto," or in the act.

Once in the hands of the National Police, the individual (suspect) had two days for preliminary inquiry and identification processing. Three more days were allowed for transfer to the Province Interrogation Center and a supplementary investigation was allowed for up to 30-days. Three more days were allocated to the Province Chief for review of the case and forwarding the dossier and case to the Province Security Committee for sentencing, release, or referral of the decision within seven days for trial by the Military Court. The Ministry of Interior had to authorize any deviation from the promulgated schedule. The total was 46 days from apprehension and arrest to trial.

9. Detainee Classification [Handbook, 15]

Detainees were to be classified as either a Prisoner of War or a Civil Defendant. VC (the combatant kind and not the VCI) and North Vietnamese Army personnel were to be "accorded PW status and treated according to the provisions of the Geneva Convention. The rest were civil defendants including all VCI. If an NVA soldier or VC found serving on the VCI were to be identified they were classified as PW's, but reported as neutralized VCI.

10. Province Security Committee [Handbook, 16]

Province Security Committees (PSC) predated the Phoenix/Phung Hoang Programs, having been established in 1957. They had a long standing experience base for processing detainees; however, the PSC was classified as an administrative and not judicial body; therefore, they had the ability to impose administrative detention, but not the judicial authority. PSCs were composed of a minimum of the following:

• Province Chief or City Mayor	Chairman
• Public Prosecutor or Judge	Legal Advisor
• Sector Commander	Member
• Province or City Council Member	Member
• National Police Chief (local)	Member
• Military Service Security Chief	Member
• Chief of Internal Security	Briefing Officer

PSCs must meet once a week to review dossiers of the suspects to make determinations of course of action to be taken. Suspect detainees were sometimes allowed to appear before the PSC, but did not have the right to do so. PSC courses of action were:

- Release if considered innocent
- Military Court: If there was sufficient evidence the case would be forwarded to the Court
- Administrative detention for up to two years if the suspect is believed to threaten national security.
- Determination of place of residency for security threats
- Forward case to a Civil Court
- Forward the case to another Province for disposition
- PW determination and transfer into PW channels
- May recommend drafting into the Army

11. An Tri Detention [Handbook, 17-18]

An-Tri detention was for the VCI cadre so identified and so proven. Mere membership or function in the VCI was a national security offense under GVN law and that membership or function could be "inferred from acts or intelligence data." Although there was "no rigid rule regarding the amount or type of evidence necessary to support an-tri-detention," obviously the more comprehensive the dossier and solid the evidence, the better the case and chance for detainment by security committees. Since this was not considered a criminal conviction "the burden of proof is less than that required by a court." Proof of VCI membership or function was sufficient to convict. Prosecutors were asked not to just quote from the dossier or target folder, but to present some form of proof or documentation of the VCI membership or function. The following were to be relied on more than just the dossier:

- Incriminating documents (enemy membership lists, correspondence, diaries, notebooks)
- Enemy weapons or material found in the possession of the accused on apprehension
- Eye witness (accomplices, accessories, "Chieu Hoi" ralliers to the government)

- Interrogation statements or confessions (cannot convict on this alone)
- Intelligence reports (hearsay included)

All of the intelligence, reports, witness statements and related materials were to be included in the dossier provided the court and "identified by number and name of source, except where there is a danger of source compromise." Once proven, "sentencing is automatic" and done according to the "Green Book," which was the list of all VCI Cadre by function and level.

The fact that interrogation statements alone were insufficient to convict was a safety precaution that is largely unrecognized by critics of Phoenix/Phung Hoang. This was also one of the hundreds of differences in how the VCI treated their prisoners and how the GVN processed their detainees.

12. In Country Training [Handbook, 19]

By the time I was assigned to the Phoenix Program the in-country training for US personnel at Vung Tau on the coast of Vietnam had been cancelled. The course was to acclimate US military advisors to Vietnam and provide a PHUNG HOANG Orientation Course designed to acquaint advisors with the GVN agencies in support of the program and the problems encountered within the program. Instead this training was incorporated into the course at Fort Bragg using native Vietnamese. Vung Tau was considered a resort and there were a lot of distractions. Perhaps that is why there was no longer an in-country phase of training.

For all GVN personnel, particularly PIOCC and DIOCC personnel, each Military Region established a course at headquarters.

13. In-Country Support [Handbook, 20-23]

Support was not what anyone could do for the advisors, but what the advisors could do for their counterparts and to support PHUNG HOANG efforts. Support by Phoenix Advisors was dependent on the Military Region and the written and oral instructions promulgated by them; however, there were commonly identified areas for support of the program in all regions. By level support was from Region down to District. By function the following were areas of support provided by advisors:

- Logistics (equipment and supplies)
- Maintenance for PHUNG HOANG centers
- Advisors and advice
- Funds
- Transportation (often acquiring a helicopter for inspections by higher headquarters)

The first two support items are directly mentioned in the Handbook. The other three are implied by the handbook or observed. The rest of the material in this section dealt with problems and difficulties and how to overcome them.

14. Publicity [Handbook, 23]

PHOENIX/PHUNG HOAG was not to become a secret clandestine program as often inferred, but was an open tool for Psychological Warfare and Psychological Operations cadre and advisors. Publicity was considered useful and advisors were to encourage both American and South Vietnamese to discuss the program and the value to the populace.

15. Operational Planning Guide [Handbook, Annex A]

The Operational Planning Guide provided the nuts and bolts of the operations to be conducted and the intelligence activities to be employed. Instructors at Fort Bragg concentrated on how to perform the tasks involved in intelligence collection and target analysis. The intelligence concept of the Area of Operations (AO) is integral to the training, but not spelled out in the Handbook. In the Handbook it is called the area of responsibility in Annex A and that is the closest to identifying the AO, other than specifying a district or province. Since this section is so important, most of the material is quoted directly from the Handbook.

I. General:
1. NP, PSB, MSS, PRU, S-2 (Intelligence section), RD (Rural Development), (as appropriate establish informant networks throughout the area of responsibility.
2. Situation section(s) develop a current counterintelligence estimate for the area (Province or District)
3. Prepare a counterintelligence collection worksheet listing all intelligence resources.
4. Develop a list of the VCI methods of operation in the area, i.e., tax collecting, proselyting, armed propaganda, terrorism in order of the VCI priority.
5. Levy specific intelligence collection requirements on specific agencies. (See Case Officer Operation)

II. Analyze the intelligence available:
1. Determine VCI patterns of activity.
2. Determine VCI routes used.
3. Determine VCI commo-liaison activity.
4. Determine VCI support activities.
5. Determine VCI probable course of action.

III. Assign Case Officers to specific areas of interest, for example,
1. VCI village organizations and activities.
2. VCI district organizations and activities.
3. VCI province organizations and activities.
4. Commo-liaison activities.
5. Terrorist activities.
6. Specific individuals.

IV. Case Officers Build Intelligence
1. VCI personality targets are assigned to case officers.
2. All available information reports, captured documents and interrogation reports on the Individual are assembled in the VCI Target Folder.
3. "VCI Target Personality Data Forms" and "Short Form Offender Dossiers" are initiated. (These forms are securely attached to the VCI Target Folders).
4. VCI Target Folders are reviewed daily by case officers who

levy Information Requirement Forms to fill the gaps on the VCI GTArget Personality Data Form and in the Short Form Offender Dossier.

5. Source reports, responses to information Requirement Forms, Captured Documents, Chieu Hoi debriefings, interrogation reports, etc., are received by case officers who extract relevant information to be posted to the "VCI Target Personality Data Forms" and "Short Forem Offender Dossiers." These reports are filed in the dossier or an Information Summary is prepared.

6. Recommendation for an operation against the target is made when the data base will ensure a reasonable chance of apprehension and conviction before the Province Security Committee.

V. Case Officers prepare initial Operations Plan to be provided the action agency. Consider the following factors:
1. The target.
2. The results required.
3. The support required from member agencies.
4. The forces available.
5. Operational security.

VI. Approval of action agency Operations Plan by PIOCC or DIOCC Chief.

VII. Conduct special training, briefings, and/or rehearsals as required.

VIII. Execute the operation.

IX. Exploit the operation and conduct critique.

X. Add intelligence to the local Data Bank.

The section goes on to explain that the Special Police are the ones who should develop the plans required and that the operational procedures should be instituted from Central to District levels. "All plans should be reviewed and approved by Province or District Chief or his appointed representative. At District level the VCI Target Folders are maintained by the District Special Police case officers. For operational security purposes the active VCI Target Folders are kept in the District Special Police office which then becomes the Political Sub-section of the Situation Section of the DIOCC."

In practice most Special Police activities were in a one room or two room building.

16. Inspection Visits [Handbook, Annex B]

GVN officials and the US Phoenix advisor were provided an inspection checklist and inspections were to be conducted from the top down. This meant the Center visited the regions, the regions visited both the provinces and districts, and provinces conducted their own inspections of the districts.

17. Fingerprinting [Handbook, Annex C]

All suspects were to be fingerprinted whether or not they were to be detained and regardless of whether or not they had a valid ID card. These fingerprints were checked with the National Police ID Service to confirm validity. The check was useful to determine if previous offenders returned to subversive activities and whether they had changed locations. There was a suppressive factor mentioned "both real and psychological, on the freedom of movement of the VCI.

18. VCI Neutralization and Identification Information System [Handbook, Annex D]

This system was composed of two reports: 1.) Biographic/Neutralization Report and 2.) Province Security Committee Processing Report.

Biographic/Neutralization Report

This report was intended to not only systematically present information on past and present offenders, but provided operational and judicial coordination potential. The Phoenix Program recognized that the VCI intentionally set separate boundaries for provinces and districts in order to move between jurisdictions and avoid either detection or capture by appropriate field forces. For example, one night the field force from one jurisdiction may have a night mission, but the one next door did not. Knowing when the RF were in force in one area, the VCI could easily slip into another and hide for the night.

Cross-referencing was made possible by the reporting and time and resources could be saved as well as coordinated actions planned by adjacent juridisdictions.

The <u>PSC Processing Report</u> was a monthly and year-to-date summary of "province-by-province VCI processed, their disposition, the rate at which they are processed, the time lapse between capture and disposition, and the number of PSC meetings.

19. Circle Trigon Paperwork Exercises

Exercises had been developed by JFK Center staff using the "Circle Trigon Party". I never understood why they did not just use the Communist Party of Vietnam, but decided perhaps the generalization was useful for other potential countries. The exercises involved perusing documents and filling out the appropriate targeting and short offender forms and then preparing operations against the suspects.

20. Vietnamese Village Field Exercise

The culmination of training was a Field Training Exercise (FieldEx) in the setting of a series of Vietnam Villages. Phoenix trainees were distributed to a series of villages, which as I recall numbered five. Roles to be played were as a VCI, fence sitters undecided as to allegiance, and GVN Officials. My role was as a VCI commo-liaison cadre, a low level position to be sure. Missions were given to VCI and GVN to recruit the fence sitters. The exercise was set up to favor the GVN forces and to provide confidence in how the program worked. The instructors for the course acted as controllers and as advisors to the province Chief. Initial contacts, who were supposed to be trustworthy and on the same side, were provided the role players. The idea was to "win the hearts and minds" of the fence sitters and convert the other side's players to either the VCI or GVN cause. I immediately set about to take over the area of operations and made good progress on Day 1 of the five day exercise having coordinated secretly with my fellow VCI and then started giving instructions as everyone else seemed to be standing around. By Day 2 I had identified and recruited half of the fence sitters and a couple of the GVN. At the end of Day 3, Captain Roger Koltz came over to me and said you have caused us to shut down the Field Exercise because you have far outmatched the GVN side. That was not supposed to happen, but that is a testament to your capabilities. This is the first time this has happened.

I graduated first in the class, not only by killing off the Field Exercise, but by having the first perfect Vietnamese language score. I knew I was going to miss Fort Bragg with the pine scent, the chow hall with all you can eat, and the Country Music playing over the tape system, "Easy Loving" with Freddie Hart and the Heartbeats.

CHAPTER 6

Anticipation

I sometimes wonder when reading accounts by other authors why none of them ever seem positive about the Vietnam War. I wanted to be in the war. I was about to miss it, but at least I would have one year. God, country, and family were extremely important to me and the best way to preserve them all was to fight the good fight. I never understood fear and anxiety in anybody, so it is difficult for me to relate to them. Perhaps war is in the genes. As a descendant of the sister of William the Conqueror and of the Earl of Warburton on one side of the family and of a Scandinavian warrior class on the other, my family history is replete with battles and campaigns. Anticipation is the best word I can use to explain my feelings about going to Vietnam. There was a heightening of sensitivity, of awareness, of excitement, and, well, yes, anticipation.

If You're Going to San Francisco

By 1972 the "Summer of Love" had turned to the winter of Haight. The hippies were all deflowered by now. Not long after Christmas with my wife, three year old daughter, and our parents and grandparents in McCamey and Ranger, Texas, we returned to the Oxford Green Apartments in Laurel, Maryland, where we were living and I reported to the Baltimore-Washington Airport for the cross-country flight to San Francisco. The plane landed in Los Angeles on its scheduled stop and then we were told an engine had to be pulled and we would not leave until late the next day. My modus operandi is to be early for any event and going to Vietnam was about as important an event as I could imagine and the flight absolutely was not to be missed.

Fortunately I was one day ahead of schedule, just in case, so then I boarded a northbound bus for San Francisco for an overnight stay and a next day flight out of Travis AFB. That meant a night in a hotel in San Francisco. I was one of those who always was trying to save the government money, so I stayed in a low cost place with not much more than a bed and a dirty high ceiling. I walked around the streets of San Francisco until it was getting dark and then went to bed. Suffice it to say I did not spend all of my per diem pay.

Arrival in Vietnam

January 17, 1972, time to report to Travis Air Force Base, Oakland, California for my tour of duty in Vietnam. I arrived at the Travis AFB Terminal in a taxi that picked me up in San Francisco. I showed my orders for Vietnam at the gate and was left off at the air terminal. I had two hours to wander around the base terminal. Captain Gunderson, Captain Rice, and Captain Chandler, some of my friends from the course at Fort Bragg joined me in the terminal and we talked about potential assignments and the prospects of the war winding down. The other three were on their second assignment to Vietnam and began to get more serious about what to expect and how we would be processed once in country.

I expected a military flight on a C-130 or some such military plane, but instead was treated to a Pan American flight with real stewardesses. The Boeing 707 used for this flight was the Intercontinental series with a longer fuselage, larger wings and Pratt & Whitney turbofan (JT3D) engines that had a cruising range of 6,000 miles. The 707 was ideal for crossing the Pacific with a stopover enroute either in Guam or Manila, Philippines. Departure was around 10 am. Seating was maxed out at 141 passengers and every seat was filled.

Most of the speculation on the flight was about the length of time we would be in Vietnam. I contributed the thought that the military personnel had already dwindled to under 140,000 and that the Republic of Vietnam had 1,000,000 men committed to the defense of the South. My only concern was staying into month 12 in order to have the tour count as a full overseas short tour on my Officer Record Brief.

Our flight stopped over at Clark AFB, Philippines for refueling and we all got off the plane and walked around the Tarmac looking out at the backwash of Manila. Someone said the Base Exchange was open in the evening just for our flight, so we all filed. The most popular item to purchase was apparently a Seiko watch. Since I normally did not wear a watch and since I thought I might have to be on time for meetings, I bought a $60 one with a cobalt blue dial.

I slept the rest of the way until the pilot announced we were approaching the coast of Vietnam and would soon fly over the resort of Vung Tau. Everyone cheered at the mention of Vung Tua, so I guessed it must be a popular place to go. International Flights arrived either at Tan Son Nhut Airbase or Bien Hoa, Saigon, South Vietnam, possibly depending on the local tactical situation. Our flight suddenly took a hard left maneuver and dropped precipitously in a tight spiral at the same time toward Tan Son Nhut. My cohorts laughed and said the situation was normal. I thought the pilot must have had combat duty but later learned that as long as the flight was over 5,000 feet it was unlikely to be shot down and once it approached that level, the shorter the time in the air the better.

January must have been a good month for acclimation. I have read numerous accounts of the stifling heat and problems adjusting. The day was sunny and warm, but not sweltering. As we filed off the plane, officers first, we were directed to a tin roof building with open sides to await further transportation to Camp Alpha, a transient barracks, or more appropriately tin sheds.

After one night at Camp Alpha, the Phoenix Advisors were sent to a hotel in Saigon for briefings, to receive our orders for in country assignment, and to fill out forms such as Election for Notification of Next of Kin USARV Form 560-R). The briefing came first and it was a general one that we had all received at the Phoenix course. Before lunch, we received our orders. I was assigned to Advisory Team 96, DRAC (MR-4) as the Legal Advisor with the Duty Military Occupation Specialty of G9666 and with an effective date of January 25, 1972. Whoever put the Notification form together was very thoughtful, since on page 2 we were given the option of notifying or not notifying our relatives of being slightly wounded or injured by enemy action. I checked the block, "I elect that my next of kin not be notified." If I was not coming home in a body bag, why worry my wife. I signed mine on January 21, 1972.

The first night in the hotel was pleasant with a nice breeze blowing on the roof. All incoming personnel were treated to a movie on the roof of the hotel as was done nightly for all personnel staying there. That night's movie was Dirty Harry with Clint Eastwood. The Armed Forces system rotated movies in and out on a regular basis, so there were always movies to watch all the way down to at least Regions. Richard Montgomery, Vic Gunderson, and Dick Rice stayed after the movie on the roof as we watched flares being dropped in the distance from the dark skies to the northwest of Saigon and listened to helicopters and aircraft taking off and landing. Richard commented that now he felt like he was back home in Vietnam. I just thought it looked like the Fourth of July without the pretty colors and just then some red and white phosphorous flares were lit. We discussed assignments with the other three congratulating me on going to the Delta of Vietnam. They said that was the best area to be assigned, except for the Province of Kien Giang, which was full of mangrove swamps and VC and the Province of An Xuyen at the Southern Tip of Vietnam on the Ca Mau Peninsula that was where former POW Major Nick Rowe was held until his escape 62 months later from the U Minh Forest (Forest of Darkness). After a half hour of talking and watching the flares, we were bored and still being tired from our flights went to bed.

I wondered why it would take three more days to get to MR-4. On the 22nd we turned in our currency for a mixture of Military Payment Certificates (MPC) and Vietnamese piasters. We could use the MPC in the post or base exchanges and the piasters on the economy. I traded in the $140 I had left after the purchase of the Seiko watch and took half of each. Next we were presented with our weapons, which included both the M16 and the Colt .45 that had been around forever. I wanted a Walther PPK or PPK/S, but the arms sergeant sniffed and said they were fresh out for now and I would have to be satisfied with the .45. The Walther PPK was popularized by James Bond movies, but it was lightweight, practical, small and sold to us at the MI Officer Basic Course. Although I was also an expert with a .45, I always was the most comfortable with the Walther PPK.

The 23rd was essentially a day off. After a one hour presentation on how to interface with the citizenry of Vietnam and having been given the <u>Advisor Handbook</u>, <u>Green Book</u>, and other tools for assessing and decimating the VCI (all of which I had brought along from Fort Bragg), we were allowed to travel around Saigon. My first impression was it beat Ciudad Juarez, Mexico. Traveling with my friends on a cyclo, which burned a mix of fuel and left a trail of blue hydrocarbons, the cylo with the four passenger cage on the back zoomed about the city with the guide trying to tell us half in English and half in Vietnamese the important buildings and sites on the way to the American Embassy.

We were invited by the Director, Phoenix Operations, CORDS, William Colby, to a discussion of our Phoenix duties and importance of the attack against the VCI. CORDS stood for Civil Operations and Revolutionary Development Support, which I had been told was an outgrowth of Civil Affairs operations after World War II, in which governments were assisted until they became fully operational in war torn Europe and the Far East.

Robert Komer was the "godfather" of Phoenix and he used it to meld together a common operational attack both from the military side and from the civilian ('Think CIA, USIA, and AID). Robert Komer was a Deputy Ambassador to Vietnam and the Deputy to COMUSMACV for CORDS. Komer firmly believed that the MACV intelligence directorate was focused on the military intelligence problem and often discounted the intelligence requirements for the pacification program and the VCI. In his opinion the CIA was best suited to work on the attack against the VCI, but he needed military resources to do so. The Phoenix Program was designed to make the two fit together by requiring military intelligence officers and NCOs to become advisors on the collection, collation, and communication of intelligence on the VCI. (These are my three C's of intelligence use.) The field units, to spearhead the attack and neutralization effort, was given to the counterterror units established by the CIA in 1965, who formed the Phung Hoang cadre and became identified as the Provisional Reconnaissance Units (PRU) in 1967.

Upon leaving the Embassy grounds, Dick Rice said he knew a good café frequented by Americans and we could have an afternoon lunch. We all climbed into another cyclo and headed for my first indigenous meal. Everything was similar to the restaurant in Fayetteville, North Carolina from the crab soup with noodles to the large plates of steaming food. I was already at home in a new culture and was testing my language capability as well. "Would you like a Ba Muoi Ba?" asked the pleasant serving girl in her white "*ao dai*," the long colorful dresses worn by the women with slits up the legs, at least among the more fashionable, but with black silk slacks underneath.

"Thirty three what?" I asked my friends. They were all laughing until they cried.

When the laughter subsided one of them said, "You graduated number one in languages from the course, but there are still some things to learn in the real world. Ba Muoi Ba is Vietnamese beer made here in Vietnam. Even the locals call it Tiger Piss!"

"No thank you," I replied in Vietnamese to the puzzled waitress. I then explained that I did not drink any alcohol and it was not just because I wanted to avoid Vietnam beer. Since then, I was amused by the movie, "Good Morning Vietnam with Robin Williams playing Adrian Cronauer, the popular radio voice of the Armed Forces Network. From the Internet I retrieved this little gem (Note the difference in spelling of Muoi or Muy—the second is the way it sounds.):

> Jimmy Wah: "Ba Muy Ba beer best beer in Vietnam."
> Garlick: "Ba Muy Ba beer only beer in Vietnam."
> Jimmy Wah: "Try it. Oh, what happened?"
> Cronauer: "What happened?"
> Jimmy Wah: "Formaldehyde. We put in just a touch of formaldehyde for flavor. Some people get
> sick, yeah. So if you have to be rushed to a hospital, then when you return, I give you a free salad."
> Cronauer: "Well, that seems fair. It really does."
> Garlick: "You'll get used to it."
> Cronauer: "Maybe."
> [Source: http://www.hark.com/clips/vwmkzgdczt-ba-muy-ba]

In the evening an orderly came around and told us to report the next morning for transportation to our respective assignments. The next day we were all bused to Bien Hoa for waiting Huey helicopters to take us to our divergent locations. On the helicopter going to the Delta were Major Coniglio, Major Bone, Preston Funkhouse, Dennis Deeny, Dennis Roeding, and me. The 70 mile (120 kilometer) trip to the southwest of Saigon took us over endless rice paddies with workers in conical hats that were difficult to distinguish from 5,000 feet up. The flight was uneventful. We settled down at Binh Thuy Air Base, which had been turned over to the Vietnamese and was just to the west of Can Tho, the Regional Capital of the Delta. Two Jeeps met us at the air field one driven by the Chief Phung Hoang translator and the other by Captain Little.

"Let's go meet the Colonel," cheerily said Captain Little with a wry smile, that I came to learn was always present as if he knew something no one else did.

CHAPTER 7

MR-4 Phoenix Team

Meet and Greet

The six newly arrived Phoenix/Phung Hoang Advisors were treated to a mad dash, or so it seemed through crowded roads and streets to the small compound housing the Regional Phoenix Headquarters on one side and the CIA on the other side. We caught glimpses of the muddy Bassac River, a distributary of the Mekong River on the left as we hurtled through the cyclos and pedestrians. This trip was more fun than the helicopter ride.

We pulled into a parking space and unloaded our packed bags and carried our weapons inside. The first floor contained several desks and three smiling girls appraising the new arrivals. Captain Little directed us up the stairs at the back of the room and told us to go left at the top. The six of us pile into a small room with four filing cabinets, four desks all pushed together and maps on the walls. Captain Little introduced us to Major Palmer, Major Varallo, Captain Plunkett and Captain Whitney. Major Palmer then introduced Sgt McClung and Sgt Huett. The door across the hall opened and Colonel Robert Cramer entered the room and shook hands with the "newbies". Colonel Cramer wore Artillery Brass and was a MATA Course Graduate handling combat affairs for CORDS at Regional Level. We were all under his command.

Colonel Cramer asked for orders and left the room with a copy from each of us. In a minute he came out and asked me to come into his office. "Your orders say you are to be the Legal Officer, but that means you are stuck at Region Headquarters. I was going to send you down to a district so you could get your Combat Infantry Badge and maybe with luck a purple heart. Why did they specify Legal Officer?"

"Well, Sir, I held not only a Top Secret clearance at NSA, but I had access to a lot of compartmented information including on the Vietnam War. I was told to tell you I cannot be sent down lower than Region level and cannot stay overnight outside of Can Tho or Saigon."

"Oh phoeey! Give me a minute."

I walked back across the hall and joined the others who wondered what was happening. I heard Colonel Cramer talking to someone on the phone and in a few minutes he came back across the hallway and announced final assignments. I remained assigned to Military Region 4 Headquarters as the Legal Officer.

Chopper rides were already scheduled for my compatriots. I bade them each well and success in neutralizing the VCI in their area of operations and promised to visit each of them during the year. Major Palmer offered me a desk and chair and began briefing me on my duties. As the new junior member of the team, I picked up all the extra duties such as Paymaster, CORDS Club Representative, and CORDS Compound Night Duty Guard Supervisor on a rotating basis. The CORDS Club I found was across the compound in the CIA building. The Eakin Compound was where I would be living and they would get me settled later for the evening. SGT McClung reported that I had a room assignment at the compound and sheets, blanket and pillow were already on the bed waiting for my arrival. After a short briefing on my duties, the MR-4 Phoenix Advisory Team took me to lunch at the CORDS Club.

CORDS Club

The Club had about a dozen tables which could seat from four to six. The Club was about half full and pleasantly decorated in greens and browns and yellows. The young waitresses were all young and apparently chosen as much for their pleasant faces as for their serving skills. One could say they were all cut from the same cloth, at least their *ao dais*

were, because they all were a Robin's egg blue. I commented on how nice they all looked in their *ao dais*. Major Varallo with a wicked grin said, "Wait until you see them in their miniskirts serving tables."

The equivalent for Miss is "Co," in Vietnamese. Co Huang was our waitress and I was introduced as the new Phung Advisor for Legal Affairs. Co Huang had a throaty alto voice and seemed to laugh at everything, probably partly as a language comprehension defense mechanism. Everyone ordered hamburgers, so I figured why mess with a good thing and ordered the same with fries. I was surprised at the amount and quality of the food.

Co Huang almost as a formality brought over the other girls one by one. Co Tu was taller than the others, was in charge of the wait staff, and was the chief bartender. Co Anh was larger boned and looked strongest of them all. Everyone called her Annie. I learned she was Cambodian and wondered what she was doing at the CORDS Club. Co Dep was the youngest, shortest, cutest, and sweetest looking waitress. Co Nhi was pretty and friendly. Everyone just called her Connie. I was happy to be the Phoenix Representative to the Club.

The American Chef was a senior sergeant from Presidio, Texas of Hispanic origin. He came out to welcome me and talked about what kind of things I would like to see on the menu. He showed me the breakfast menu that had steak and huevos rancheros, chorizo with eggs, and a delicious burrito. The club was in good hands.

The American Civilian contingent came by the table and Major Varallo introduced several of them to me. Once they were seated he whispered, "Esso dealers!" I guessed the meaning of his terms immediately. They likely were CIA, National Police Advisors, or Rural Development Specialists. One came by the table and shook hands with Major Varallo as if they were old buddies. Major Varallo introduced his as the "Mad Hungarian."

"Why is he mad?" I asked.

"Because he will chew the porcelain off a plate or cup and swallow it," replied Major Varallo.

"I guess that qualifies," I laughed suspiciously.

"Oh, I have stopped doing that,' said the Mad Hungarian, who I appraised at about 50 years old with high swept back slightly reddish, grayish, and blackish hair. "It was bad for my stomach and my doctor told me to stop."

CORDS Compound

We left the Phoenix Headquarters around 6 pm and arrived in darkness at Eakin Compound. The Night Duty Officer had me on a quarters list and I headed for my bunk. He handed me two types of pills and said to start taking them to prevent Malaria. Captain Little was in the bottom bunk and I was happy to be in the upper bunk with better airflow through the screened in room. I made sure no mosquitoes followed me into the room and shut the door to consider my lot. I was always thankful for the small things in life such as being in the Phoenix Program, being stationed in Can Tho at Regional Headquarters, and having a top bunk. I was blessed and ready for a good night sleep. I prayed Charlie (the term for the Viet Cong) was nowhere around, made my bed, and went to sleep.

Day two of duty began with Reveille at six, a rush to the latrines to shave, shower, and relieve myself. The place was not crowded and I began to realize the benefits of being on the downside of troop deployment in Vietnam, since advisors were also leaving and not being replaced. The compound had a mess hall where I had bacon, eggs, and sausage with milk for breakfast. Captain Ralph Little guided me to the mess hall and was responsible for driving me to work. Ralph had use of an old black painted Jeep that was left for Phoenix to use from one of the other advisory groups and drove me to pick up Captain Puckett and Major Palmer in a small hotel a few blocks north of Eakin Compound. Major Varallo and Sgt McClung had use of another vehicle that looked new and was a bright green and they had Colonel Cramer with them. I was surprised that three members of the Phoenix Advisory Group lived on the economy, but realized that was how the entire team probably lived until recently in the war.

My goal was to find out how to make the move to the hotel and live on the economy. Absorption of a culture and language is assisted by living in proximity to the natives and my desire was to attain the highest level of understanding I could. Ralph drove me to the CORDS Headquarters, but then told me to stay with the Jeep, since we were going to the morning Deputy for CORDS Briefing where he would show me how to perform translation work, just in case I might be needed. I did not enlighten Ralph as to my language ability, or at least tested ability.

First real day on the job and SGT McClung asks me if I know the Army Functional Filing System. I said I had not had the opportunity of serving in a regular military unit and would he please explain it to me.

"With pleasure," smiled SGT McClung. "You have to know the

system, since I expect you to be one of the last ones out of here and it is never too early to train in functional files management."

"I agree, lead on McClung."

Rather than bore you with the filing system that the Army created and businesses now use with a three digit initial code such as 100 series for Administrative Files, I will simply tell you that with the decimals after the series number and with writing on the right hand side of the page the file number to which a document must be posted is wonderful. Not only can everyone readily understand it, they are functional within the first hour of training. One key to the system is a chronological correspondence log cross referenced with documents in the other files. One can always find a document that had been sent or received and those were usually the ones everyone wanted to see in the future.

Everyone was still gone. "Now what do we do, SGT McClung?"

"Now we begin preparing the Phoenix Regional Report to send to Saigon," replied SGT McClung. Ralph had given me the results of the morning briefing, SGT McClung showed me the forms to be completed, and I began filling them out. I presumed the Vietnamese were doing the same thing and hoped they matched when they all got to Saigon. I saved the report for COL Cramer to review prior to sending. COL Kelleher, whom I had met in Saigon, was the person to whom the report was addressed and sent out in a message pouch, probably by daily helicopter traffic.

"Where is my counterpart?" I asked SGT McClung.

"You are the Legal Advisor. You don't get one, for now. What you do get to do is plan inspection visits, order the helicopters, and go on them with one of the majors or COL Cramer. You will be plenty busy doing that. I hope you have better Vietnamese language skills than the last bunch we had here. It comes in handy for explaining to the COL what they are saying. Start reading the briefing materials in the packets I laid on your desk and learn the forms that they use to make their briefing boards in the provinces and districts. That will help a lot."

I began my memorization projects. COL Cramer came in and said, "Tomorrow I want you to go with Captain Little and Captain Puckett to the Vietnamese Phung Hoang Office Compound and meet the Regional Vietnamese Phung Hoang Chief, Major Thieu (alternate name). Captain Little and Captain Puckett will show you their desk in his office and go over the forms. Major Thieu will want to brief you in

Vietnamese to test your language capability. Don't worry, none of us have done very well there talking Vietnamese with him, but he speaks good English."

"I will do my best, sir."

"That is all I expect," said COL Cramer.

I thought to myself, this is the first reasonable artillery officer I have met, but why is an artillery Colonel in charge of the Phoenix program in the Delta?

CHAPTER 8

On the Job Training in Military Region 4

MR-4 was often referred to as the Delta Regional Assistance Command (DRAC). The other regions were called by their number, but the Delta had special status. The greatest population, the most hectares under cultivation, the more rice production, and the best land distribution was in the Delta. The Mekong River produced the Delta with vast flow of silt exiting the Asian mainland and laying down fertile layers of soil that made perfect rice paddies.

The Delta was composed of 16 provinces. Each Province was rated for security conditions under the Hamlet Evaluation System (HES), using a form called the Hamlet Evaluation Survey. The HES Report sent every month to Saigon rated each hamlet from A as most secure from VC influence or members down to categories D and E with more than 50% of the population probably VC. Those simply controlled by the VC for an extended period were classified as V. One report I wrote down in April listed the Provinces alphabetically and then in rank order by reported security situation for the Vietnamese. I composed a chart with the security rankings, population statistics, and Capital Cities of the Provinces to help me get a picture of the needs of the Delta Phung Hoang Program.

The estimated population of the Delta was 6,847,400 give or take a few infiltrators from the NVA. Cultivated land dedicated to rice paddies was estimated by USAID, Land Reform Division in May 1972 at 1,639,609 hectares and land listed as other agricultural uses was 104,475 for a total for cultivated land of 1,744,354 hectares or almost 94%. [Population: HES Report, April 1972/ Land use: USAID/Land Reform Tabulation, May 1972.]

Delta Provinces Ranked in Order
Most to Least Secure April 1972*

Rank	Province	Population	Capital City
1	An Giang	618,200	Long Xuyen
2	Go Cong	203,300	Go Cong
3	Sa Dec	317,100	Sa Dec
4	Kien Tuong	54,100	Moc Hoa
5	Chau Doc	581,400	Chau Phu
6	Kien Phong	408,200	Cao Lanh
7	Ba Xuyen	455,600	Bac Lieu
8	Dinh Tuong	607,500	My Tho
9	Phong Dinh	534,300	Can Tho
10	Bac Lieu	352,000	Soc Trang
11	Vinh Long	577,900	Vinh Long
12	Kien Giang	495,200	Rach Gia
13	Vinh Binh	414,500	Truc Giang
14	Chuong Thien	290,700	Vi Thanh
15	Kien Hoa	629,800	Ben Tre
16	An Xuyen	307,600	Quan Long

*HES Report, April 1972
http://upload.wikimedia.org/wikipedia/commons/2/2d/Southvietmap.jpg

Major General Thomas N. Tarpley, Commander
Delta Regional Assistance Command

Major General Tarpley was briefed every morning at CORDS Headquarters by one of the Phoenix advisors providing the interpretation from Vietnamese into English. Ralph Little had the duty the first day I was sent to accompany him to learn the process. Ralph explained that before the briefing he would get a pre-brief from the Senior Vietnamese Commander or his Deputy, write down the statistics and simply follow them on the board as he briefed the DRAC Commander and the Deputy for CORDS, Willie Wilson among other assorted American advisors. Ralph said he spoke little Vietnamese, but had a translation sheet and they always followed the same format.

I went into the sound proof booth with him as he listened on the headphones and watched the chart through the narrow and grimy glass. I had a hard time seeing the numbers, but Ralph seemed to follow along appropriately. Ralph simply had to track the numbers and conversation, but without seeing the board, there was the potential for problems. I filed that away for future reference. This day the briefing went smoothly as the VCI activities and neutralization counts were covered followed by GVN losses either by killing, wounding, or probable defection to the VC. Ralph drove me back to the Headquarters and put me in the hands of SGT McClung. Apparently everyone else was out somewhere. Inspections? Coffee? Important meeting? Wandering around?

After the briefing, I was introduced to General Tarpley by COL Cramer as the new Phoenix Legal Advisor. General Tarpley said he would use me when they needed a legal opinion on activities within the region. I did not say anything about my language capability. There was no time to do so.

Major General Tarpley was the Advisor to Lt. Gen. Ngo Quang Truong, Commander IV Corps (Vietnamese Regional Division designation) a highly capable combat leader and under whose leadership in 1971, the Delta had increasing success in both the conventional fighting with units and in the unconventional war with guerrilla fighters, the Viet Cong. In May 1972, he was replaced by Major General Nguyen Vinh Nghi. LT GEN Truong, the predecessor to MG Nghi stated,

"(MG Nghi) proved to be the man for this challenge because of his familiarity with the Mekong Delta. His actions were timely and responsive. A cautious man by nature, he nevertheless accepted reasonable risks whenever required in order to resolve combat situations. His energetic drive and talent for maneuver left an excellent impression on his adviser, Major General Thomas M. Tarpely, DRAC commander. They worked hand in hand in close association in almost every situation to ensure that the Delta remained secure during the enemy offensive."

Coal Bin Willie, Deputy for CORDS

The Deputy for CORDS (DEPCORDS), MR-4 had an interesting history. Wilbur Wilson had the nickname, "Coal Bin Willie." I asked Captain Little why he had the nickname. Ralph said the story went that he was a Colonel at Fort Knox, Kentucky. I had an affinity for Fort Knox having my combat training as a Tank Commander in the Armor Basic Course as my first introduction to Army life. Ralph explained that all the coal bins for the buildings were painted white and had to be kept clean of coal dust. Colonel Wilson would put on white gloves and rub each coal bin. If his gloves got dirty, there was hell to pay for the offending Officers and NCOs associated with the building.

Major Thieu, How Do You Do

Ralph next took me to see the person Phoenix advised at the Phung Hoang Offices, Major Thieu (alternate name for protection). Major Thieu had a toothy smile, but I could tell he had a hard core center beneath the pleasant exterior. He was extremely polite and introduced me to the members of his team. Major Thieu said he understood advisors could no longer go on patrols with his men and expressed his sorrow over that fact. He was accustomed to dealing with Americans and was not the touchy feely type, which pleased me greatly. I did not want to hold hands. The handshake was perfunctory and done in one up and down motion before he withdrew. Good, I thought.

Ralph showed me to the desk he occupied when he came over daily and the stacks of documents and reports he reviewed from all the Provinces. There were 16 Provinces in the Delta and a surprising number of VC controlled areas with the worst in 1972 being An Xuyen Province in the far south where the U Minh Forest was the most dense. I was shown a security chart based on the Hamlet.

John Paul Vann

John Paul Vann was a Phoenix legend who I had the opportunity to meet at CORDS headquarters in Can Tho one day in early 1972. The stories I heard included him dressing in black pajamas, as the VC night pants and shirt were black, and traveling about MR III on motor bike, or joining raiding parties. The one thing I had heard though was that he slept only two hours a night. I just had to ask how he did that. He told me, "Son, I usually sleep four hours a night, but sometimes two. I trained myself to do that, so I would have more time to work. I do take an afternoon power nap of about 15 minutes."

John Paul Vann was one of those persons you thought must be invincible for the number of operations he personally conducted or accompanied and for the love of killing the VC day or night in combat situations. I hated the announcement that on June 9, 1972, Senior Military Advisor for CORDS, MR-3 was killed in a helicopter crash near Pleiku while assisting South Vietnamese troops in the defense of Kontum.

I started to practice sleeping four hours a night and then working, exercising, studying, or doing something productive with my new extra time. Forty years later I still wake up in four hours, but can usually find a way to go back to sleep for a couple more hours after doing some work in the middle of the night. I do take more than 15 minute naps in the afternoon, though.

John Paul Vann was a straight shooter and a person who at the least would outwork everyone else. I modeled my future behavior on his patterns.

Chuong Thien

Chuong Thien was the target of my first assist on a Phoenix inspection. Colonel Cramer went along with me to show me how to ask the right questions of the Vietnamese and of the Provincial Phoenix Officer. I loved the perfect weather flight down to the Capital City of Chuong Thien, which was Vi Thanh. The Phoenix Advisor was Captain Dennis Roeding from my Phoenix class, so I took along a couple of useful gifts from the Post Exchange. Dennis opened up to me on what it was like to serve in a jungle environment with mosquitoes everywhere and with a Vietnamese counterpart that loved to go out on night patrols to different sections of Chuong Thien. Chuong Thien as I learned was a Province that at times was very active with VC incidents.

From my notes in the Chuong Thien Target Folder I found that in August 1968, the Joint Prisoner Rescue Command coordinated a rescue effort in the Province named Operation CRANBERRY BOG.

The 135th MI Group in Can Tho reported that two Vietnamese escaped from a POW camp in Chuong Thien and that it held eight Americans and 35 Vietnamese. There were reports that 1LT Nick Rowe who had been captured five years earlier was alive and possibly at this VC prison compound identified for this particular raid. The Army of the Republic of Vietnam's 21st ARVN Division declined to launch the raid, so U.S. Air Force Captain David McNabb mounted the raid with the American PRU Advisor (a Navy SEAL), two escapees from the compound, and nine Province Reconnaissance Unit raiders. Operating after midnight on August 28th, the raiding party crossed a river and attacked at dawn killing two VC guards. The others ran. The results of the raid were to free 49 Vietnamese POWs of the VC. They were ARVN soldiers shackled and standing in chest-deep water. [The source for this information is from old notes I had and double checked http://www.flyarmy.org/panel/battle/68082801.HTM]

My Tho

I conducted my first visit alone to My Tho, where my good friend Major Coniglio was the Province Phoenix/Phung Hoang Advisor. I looked forward to testing my Vietnamese language in a pure setting and the visit to the Province Intelligence Operations Center (PIOC) proved to be a challenge in communication, but rewarding as well. The helicopter pilot met me at the hotel where Major Coniglio was staying and said he had to fly off on a mission and would send another bird in the morning. I called Colonel Cramer and told him that I had to spend the night in My Tho and he said fine. I suppose he was laughing that I had to stay in Dinh Tuong Province overnight, when I was supposed to never stay outside of Can Tho.

"Have you ever driven along the highway along the rice paddies? Asked Major Coniglio. "No, but it sounds like fun."

Late in the afternoon we traveled down the highway with Major Coniglio driving. As we approached a change from one paddy to another we heard a couple of pings.

"Did you hear those?" Asked Major Coniglio.

""Yes, they sounded like pings," I said.

"Those were bullets, Roy."

We pulled out two M16s and scanned the area from the Jeep, but saw nothing.

"You have a scratch on your right arm," he said.

"It must have been from grabbing the rifle so fast," I said.

"I think you may have been grazed by a bullet," he said.

"No, I don't think so. It's just a small scratch."

Major Coniglio pulled out a first aid kit and I swabbed the scratch and put a band aid on it. We never talked about it again, but I was possibly entitled to a purple heart. I did not want one, because I thought it might be a sign of weakness and I certainly did not have incontrovertible evidence that it was a bullet that made the scratch. Major Coniglio turned around and we headed back to My Tho for the evening.

Major Coniglio got me a room at the hotel and we settled in for a good meal and then I went to bed. In the middle of the night I awoke to see a lizard staring at me from near the ceiling. I shooed the lizard away and went back to sleep. The helicopter came about 1000 the next morning and I returned to Can Tho.

Postscript: In July, Major Coniglio was wounded traveling along the road at a location he said we were at back in February when he thought we were shot at. He made it back to My Tho on his own and I visited him again in August.

Night Duty

My first night duty at Eakin Compound was early in my tour. Every 27 days I would have night duty at the compound. After 6 pm, I was in charge and assembled the American's who were to guard the compound that night. One was missing. I alerted the LTC in charge of the compound. He checked the list and took me with him to the room of the tardy guard. We found the guard was bombed out of his mind with drugs, so we called on the alternate and I went about my business of placing them in the watchtowers with a Vietnamese guard in each one. I was certain the delinquent guard would be court-martialed. During the night I walked the compound every hour checking to insure the guards were awake. On one of my visits to one end of the compound, I hear two shots ring out on the other side. I rushed to the location of the shooting and hollered up, "Did you shoot an infiltrator?"

The response came back, "Yeah, we did. It was a big rat."

I was happy that guard duty came around only once a month, although by July it was reduced time between night duty shifts with more personnel leaving Vietnam.

Paymaster

Paymaster was another distasteful duty. On the first day I was made paymaster, I was given brown bags full of Vietnamese currency and Military Payment Certificates and had to count them all before going down the list and counting out the right amount to every soldier. I was told that if any money was missing from the count to the count out, I would get to repay it from personal funds. I was very careful that each bill was separated and had the use of gummed finger covers or whatever they are called to assist me. I was happy to say all the counts were accurate and I did not have to put any money into the kitty.

Recreation

Captain Spencer and Major Denny Monroe were two of my good friends. Captain Spencer and I often played a wicked game of tennis at Eakin Compound in the evening under the lights. One night I was particularly irritated at losing a game and threw my racket. The racket sailed over the fence, chopped through the leaf of a banana tree and landed on the tin roof of the LTC in charge of the compound. He came running out and asked if there was incoming mortar fire. I sheepishly explained that I was angry at losing a close game and threw my tennis racket. After a short admonishment, we all laughed together and I never threw my racket again.

Captain Spencer later lost his life in a plane crash near Soc Trang and I stopped playing tennis. I moved on to handball.

Major Monroe was a good friend to have because he was in the Quartermaster Corps and had the only air conditioned personal room on the compound as far as I knew, but I never strayed into the rooms of the Lieutenant Colonels and Colonels. On occasion we would talk about the war and life in general in his pleasant climate controlled room.

The Eakin Compound and the CORDS Compound that housed the DEPCORDS and Generals had a swimming pool. Let me correct that. Both compounds had a water reservoir encased in concrete and tile in which we could swim. I learned that CORDS leadership was very clever in asking for the water reservoir and having it built by the SeaBees, the Construction Battalion of the Navy. I hoped there were filters and sufficient chlorine to kill whatever was tracked into the pool/reservoir.

Tet a Tet

Tet is the accepted version of New Years in Vietnam and corresponds to the Chinese lunar New Year rather than the Gregorian calendar that still has not penetrated the consciousness of the agrarian Vietnamese nor replaced the traditional holiday of celebration among the city dwellers. Dancing tigers and dragons roam the streets either in parades or impromptu celebration while firecrackers and fireworks are lit.

Within the family unit, Tet means three days of peace and harmony. Depending on the year Tet falls between the last two weeks of January and the first two weeks of February, so we can take February 1 as the average date. The cultural harmony is observed for three days by everyone in the family and to those outside the family, since it is unlucky for the next twelve months to be rude to anyone or quarrel within the family. The psychological impact is to renew the spirit and allow all work to cease, both to give the land a rest and the laborer. Extended family members usually congregate under the roof of the primary family unit as best they can. Joss sticks are lit and the smell of incense pervades not only the house but the streets. You can smell Tet.

Ancestors are cared for at the cemeteries and their burial plots are tidied up. After Tet, the first of anything, such as a purchase, seal on a document, or tilling the soil is done in a ceremonial way according to the tradition of the trade.

Small red flimsy paper envelopes are exchanged not only with in the family, but especially with children and people that are well-liked outside the family unit. The girls at the CORDS Club provided the envelopes for us to gift them as they gifted us with a small unit of paper money as a way to be friendly and as a way to demonstrate generosity, I suppose in case the gods are watching.

Intelligence had some inkling that the NVA and VC might attack again on Tet as they did in 1968 and indeed troop movements with heavy duty conventional equipment were moving to the borders all around South Vietnam. Tet came and went in 1972 without major incident.

Tet Treat

Sometime around or during Tet the American Phoenix Team was treated to a special Tet meal at one of the restaurants in Can Tho with the Vietnames counterparts hosting. As the last of the likely advisors to be sent to the Delta, I was the focus of attention and had to sample the food first and say how much I enjoyed it. I was prepared for this from the MASA course and knew that I would have some strange delicacies. The first course tasted like salted peanuts and cracked like pork rinds. This was fried bird's beaks. The soup was interesting with everyone receiving a bowl of broth with on big white lump in the middle. The broth was fine, but one had to chew the white lump after cutting it up with a knife. That was the Sea Slug Soup. The rest of the meal was excellent, since the Vietnamese always had more gravies with their dishes than the more watery Chinese versions of the same dish.

How to Lose Your Pants

Not only was I feeling good in February, I was feeling immortal. On Saturday afternoon I decided to walk the streets of Can Tho to see all the shops and things going on. More than that I wanted the Vietnamese to see the rare American willing to walk into their midst, since the rest I had observed would drive just to one shop to buy something and leave. My wife had sent me two pairs of double knit pants with pockets in the front instead of the back. I thought that was a great idea, so I could keep my hands on my wallet as I walked.

I drove to the most densely populate shopping area I could find, got out of the car and began my stroll, looking in the windows of small shops. In a few minutes I was surrounded by about eight small boys that I took just to be interested children. All of a sudden, however, I found my pants pockets were ripped to let my wallet fall out, but a few strands of the double knit threads held. One kid then tried to pop my watch off my wrist in an instant, but I was too fast. I caught his hand in one of mine and the falling watch in the other. The locals were both amused and astonished as well as concerned for someone, but the question was for the boy or for me. In any event I held both my watch and wallet and with purposeful strides, but without panic returned to my Jeep and decided to not stroll the streets of Can Tho again, at least not alone. I felt safer attacking the VCI.

CHAPTER 9

Vietnamization,
January-February 1972

Map 18 — Enemy Attacks in MR-4

Phoenix MR-4

According to the Phoenix MR-4 Advisor Team members, MAJ Varallo and MAJ Palmer in particular, January and February were relatively quiet in terms of VC activity and the goals of VCI neutralization were not being met in the Districts and Provinces. The team was uncertain what this all meant, but welcomed the respite for the sake of the Delta population. They cheerily told me not to worry, things will probably pick up in the spring and we will all be extremely busy.

"Vietnamization" was the term used starting in 1968 by the military for turning over military equipment, assets, intelligence functions, and operational responsibility with American support to the Vietnamese. As American forces continued their withdrawal in 1972, increasing emphasis was placed on the Army of the Republic of Vietnam (ARVN) performing their tasks in an aggressive manner, and charging the National Police and the PRU, PSDF, and RF/PF with taking over raids against the VCI. There was uneven performance at best with some ARVN units and their commanders dodging the VC as much as taking them on in combat.

The Delta, though, was a success story by January 1972. VC had been systematically hunted down and neutralized. That did not mean that NVA and VC forces had disappeared from the Delta. They simply were regrouping and licking their wounds from 1971.

When I use the term Delta, I am referring to several things. The Mekong Delta with its distributary, the Bassac or Ba Sac, depending on who is spelling it and everything south of Saigon constitutes the "Delta". The land is flat and rarely rises more than 10 feet above sea level, except for the few mountains near the Cambodian border. This extensive alluvial plain is mostly uncovered rice paddies with intermittent mangrove swamps and jungle vegetation. Canals both natural, artificial and connecting provided the water for the rice paddies.

The monsoon season from July to October turned the Delta into a vast mud pot. The VC used small isolated uncultivated area as their base of operations, while the NVA units congregated around the periphery near the border with Cambodia, in the U Minh Forest area at the bottom of the Ca Mau Peninsula and in three locations along the upper Delta coast.

The American Command structure usually called it the Delta Regional Assistance Command (DRAC), but it was CORDS MR IV or MR-4 Region, headquartered in Can Tho. The Delta was the most populated region with about two-thirds of the population of South Vietnam living there and had the best land for rice paddies which coincidentally produced about two-thirds of the rice of South Vietnam. The fact that land had been broken up from rich owners in the past and redistributed gave villagers and hamleters (a new word) a stake in the land. The fact that the early break up was caused by communists was somewhat lost on the population. USAID Land Reform concentrated on the Land To The Tiller (LTTT) Program to reinforce a stake in the land and negate one of the causes for dissatisfaction of the population. According to reports and statistical analysis this indeed was a stabilizing pacification program.

Vietnamization was now regarded as a necessity, whereas with American units everywhere it was more a concept than a reality. By 1972, the stark reality of American troop departures was beginning to sink in to the Vietnamese. The economy was becoming affected as well with the drying up of Americans spending their wages on all the fun things they could dream about to do.

The Delta was in a better position to absorb Vietnamization than the other three military regions. Even with the tremendous buildup of American troop strength, the ARVN IV Corps had three infantry divisions, two mobile groups and six ranger groups. Regional territorial forces were 200,000 and operated all over the Delta in conjunction with the PRU and other paramilitary units. The regional forces totaled about the same strength as the rest of the regions combined.

I tried to figure out strategically the stationing of the divisions. The 7th ARVN Division was located in Dinh Tuong Province around My Tho. I decided they were there to provide a centralized location from which they could be committed in the least amount of time to any sector of the Delta. The 9th Division located in Sa Dec made sense as a potential blocking force against NVA incursions from Cambodia. The one I could not figure out was the 21st Division located in Bac Lieu with the usual area of operations on the Ca Mau Peninsula. I thought they should have penetrated deeper on the Ca Mau Peninsula, or perhaps directly south of Can Tho in Chuong Thien Province. Combat operations in the Delta were always the primary responsibility of the ARVN divisions even at the apex of American combat support and advisory effort.

SITREP (Situation Report) February 1972

If I had prepared a Situation Report (SITREP in military parlance) at the end of February, beginning of March 1972, I would have said something like the following:

1. Enemy Forces: 1st Division NVA remains broken down into

small units and a majority has withdrawn deeper into Cambodia as a result of the heavy losses inflicted on them after enemy sanctuaries in Cambodia were finally eliminated in 1970 and 1971. Resupply from the sea had been interdicted causing further degradation of effort. Most of the mini-bases that remained behind were significantly penetrated and destroyed in 1971.

2. Friendly Forces: IV Corps GVN forces that were under siege in 1970 have taken the offensive. The ARVN established a new system of outposts in 1971 to maintain GVN control in formerly contested areas of the Delta that were long held by enemy forces.

3. Pacification Effort: The extensive enemy attacks in the Delta on the pacification programs and the shellings of hamlets and villages going over to the GVN because of the Central Office for South Vietnam (COSVN, the communist shadow government headquarters) orders in the form of a Resolution to attack in the Mekong Delta were blunted with the NVA suffering heavy casualties. As a result pacification is not only back on track, but accelerating as the GVN control is becoming more visible to the Delta population.

Land To The Tiller and Hamlet-Self Help initiatives of the GVN were successful throughout the Delta reducing or eliminating dependency on the VC and converting their propaganda campaigns into lies.

The GVN initiated a four year plan in early March 1972 for Community Defense and Local Self Development that offered future prospects of prosperity and security.

4. Successes: Heavy enemy fortifications in the That Son or Seven Mountain region along the Cambodian border were neutralized by the 9th ARVN Division. Enemy sanctuaries and installations in the U Minh Forest were largely destroyed by the 21st ARVN Division. The 7th ARVN Division along with territorial forces successfully neutralized enemy influence along the boundary of Dinh Tuong and Kien Phong Provinces in an area known as Base Area 470. The cradle of Viet Cong insurgency, Kien Hoa Province, where my friend Major Bone was located along with Captain Dennis Deeny, was the target of a major pacification campaign that was successful in eliminating a significant number of VCI and changing the area over to the GVN.

5. Security Situation: 95% of the Delta population now live in secure villages and hamlets.
6. Economic Situation: Rice production has increased substantially.
7. Education: Now available for every child.

From this SITREP, Vietnamization was working very well in the Delta and presaged a future of pacification and security for the populace. The Viet Cong and NVA could not allow that to happen. Intelligence indicated that the NVA and VC were working to build up supplies of arms, ammunition, and food in their remaining base areas in the U Minh Forest and Dinh Tuong Province. Enemy activity for the most part involved outpost harassment, small unit raids, and road interdictions such as blowing up a bridge here and there. Six depleted VC local force regiments were operating from their base areas. The 1st NVA Division was beyond the Cambodian border somewhere, though by March, intelligence indicated they were positioning themselves farther south than usual. [Truong, 142] LT GEN Truong in a Monograph provides a close look at the assigned forces of the GVN going into March:

> During this time, the defense of the border for MR-4 was assigned to the 44th Special Tactical Zone (STZ) whose border ranger and armor forces were deployed as a screen along the Cambodian border from the Mo Vet (Parrot's Beak) area to the Gulf of Siam. In addition to its territorial defense responsibility inside MR-4, the 44th STZ also operationally controlled two major bases in Cambodia, Neak Luong, at Route QL-l ferry crossing of the Mekong River, and Kompong Trach, some 20 km north of Ha Tien. Both bases were secured by ARVN ranger forces. The 9th ARVN Division was then conducting operations in the upper U Minh area and in Chuong Thien Province while the 21st Division operated in the lower U Minh area and in the southern portion of Cape Ca Mau. Meanwhile, the 7th ARVN Division was responsible for the two contested areas of MR-4, Dinh Tuong and Kien Hoa Provinces, and other provinces sandwiched between the Mekong and Bassac Rivers.

[Source: LT GEN Ngo Quang Truong. Indochina Monographs. THE EASTER OFFENSIVE OF 1972. U.S. Army Center of Military History.]

I apparently arrived in a convenient interlude in the war and took advantage of it by studying enemy deployments, intelligence reports, target folders, pacification statistics and maps, and everything I could learn about the Delta and the VCI.

American Drawdown

U.S. troop strength in Vietnam dropped to 136,500 by 31 January 1972, to 119,600 by 29 February, and then to 95,500 by the end of March. The North Vietnamese aided by their VCI reporting system noticed the American drawdown as well and decided that a good time to attack was while the Americans were leaving. Thus began the "Easter Campaign."

http://www.history.army.mil/html/reference/army_flag/vn.html

CHAPTER 10

NVA/VCI and the Easter Offensive,
March-April 1972

March and April are dry seasons in the Delta of Vietnam and the most conducive to night movements along the roads and rice paddy dikes. Intelligence picked up on the movement of two regiments of the enemy, probably both NVA and VC leaving the U Minh Forest and entering Chuong Thien Province directly south of Can Tho. The VCI must not have gotten any Easter eggs and were mad about it, so they decided to gain attention. Militarily the NVA and VCI made major operational and tactical mistakes and paid a heavy price. Politically North Vietnam gained their objectives once again. The idea must have been even if we lose the battles, we will win the peace.

Forget the Easter Eggs. Let's Hunt for VC

Easter Sunday was April 2, 1972. The first engagement in the campaign laid out by the North Vietnamese military leaders began 11 days earlier on March 22, 1972 with a combat engagement in Cambodia at a small Cambodian village named Kompong Trach, about 9 miles north and slightly west of Ha Tien in Kien Giang. If a line were drawn directly west into Cambodia that separated Chau Doc and Kien Giang Provinces in Vietnam, it would have come close to the location of the action.

After the earlier incursions into Cambodia, the Vietnamese IV Corps had an operational base (OB) nearby controlling one of the major NVA supply routes for weapons and infiltrating personnel entering the Delta of Vietnam. Although this kicked off the fighting as both the NVA and ARVN poured in units to the battle, the timing was premature for the NVA. The plan apparently was to continue moving units for another week or two and continuing to make adequate supply provisions for a major Easter offensive. [Truong, 144]

According to descriptions coming into the Delta Tactical Operations Center (DTOC), fighting was fierce an prolonged. In fact it lasted for a month as continual reinforcements were provided by both the ARVN and the 7th Division with their cavalry squadron along with another three committed cavalry squadrons drawn from other forces and the NVA that had one Regiment under siege and brought in two regiments that were on their way to MR IV along with elements of the 1st NVA Division that the NVA did not want to use. After fierce fighting, the ARVN units moved back from the village area defensive positions, but not before inflicting devastating losses on the NVA. B-52's resumed their strikes on the enemy positions in support of the ARVN and their bombing was critical to the devastation of the NVA.

As LT GEN Truong describes the results:

> In spite of heavy losses incurred by both sides and the fact that eventually the ARVN base at Kompong Trach had to be evacuated, this battle resulted in a major defeat for the enemy. For one thing, the 1st NVA Division, which was the enemy's single division size unit committed to the Mekong Delta at that time, had been forced to exhaust its combat potential on Cambodian soil whereas it was apparently needed to conduct major actions inside MR-4 in concert with the offensive in other areas of South Vietnam. Fighting this battle, the enemy did not succeed in breaking the household china, his primary objective; he managed only to cause minor damage to the outer fence. In other words, his mission to destroy the pacification progress in IV Corps was unsuccessful; he caused only minor disruption. Even then, the price he had to pay for it was outrageously high. The hugh losses which had been inflicted on him by our armor firepower and the devastating U.S. and VNAF airstrikes during his massive infantry assaults finally

reduced the 1st NVA Division into a unit that was no longer combat worthy for the rest of the offensive. [Truong, 144]

The ARVN eventually withdrew because the area of operations was outside normal supply lines and it was difficult to move troops and supplies in and out. The NVA could not move out because they basically had nowhere else to go. They could not go back to the north, could not move to the south, and were in Cambodia facing the possibility of hostile Cambodian unit activity. Any withdrawal by the ARVN was celebrated by propagandists as breaking the will of the GVN even after a massive defeat. That is exactly what happened. Although militarily a disaster in that the 1st NVA Division was reduced to small elements and losses were extremely high, not completing the battle was a mistake. The bright spot was that for a change the battle took place on territory outside the borders of Vietnam and did not damage civilian pacification, which was one of the stated goals of the NVA military. [Source: LT GEN Ngo Quang Truong. Indochina Monographs. THE EASTER OFFENSIVE OF 1972. U.S. Army Center of Military History.]

Phoenix/Phung Hoang Briefing Notes

Phoenix/Phung Hoang Notes are not the same as ARVN or regular army notes. Phoenix/Phung Hoang notes are from the briefings by the ARVN Commander, G2, G3, and National Police, at the Delta Tactical Operations Center (DTOC) and are operations and results of non-regular forces in support of the attack against the VCI. I began providing translations at the morning briefings on most occasions in April. Someone had discovered I did know more Vietnamese than even seasoned veterans in the field.

Starting on April 5, 1972, I have notes saved from the DTOC briefings as I was made the Assistant Operations Officer to Major Donald M. Palmer and began doing the translating for the Phung Hoang portion of the morning briefing to General Tarpley. From a short summary version on April 5, I shortly moved to a more detailed set of notes by Province and down to District level in an effort to present a better pattern analysis picture of where resources were needed so that COL Cramer could provide better advice to his counterpart. For example, on April 5, there were 150 Total Operations. I listed 23 VCI neutralized in the Delta of the Class A and B categories with 5 killed, 6 captured, and 12 ralliers (Chieu Hoi Program). On April 8, there were 100 operations. I listed total neutralizations at 34 with 13 killed, 15 captured, and 6 ralliers.

In the footnote to the April 8 statistics, I showed the My Tho City Chieu Hoi Center received four rounds of 82 mm mortar shells and the Bac Lieu Airfield received three rounds of 82 mm mortar shells. There were 74 incidents reported in the Delta including five in Cambodia. Chuong Thien had the most incidents briefed with a total of 13. The majority of the incidents were Observation Post attacks.

My April 11 notes showed there were 102 Total Operations with 24 neutralizations with 3 killed, 14 captured, and 6 ralliers. Note: One of the 24 neutralized was the capture of a Region Level Sapper Cadre in Dinh Tuong Province. I then footnoted the G2 Briefing results in which 39 incidents were reported of which 15 or about 40% were in Chuong Thien. Four of the 15 attacks in Chuong Thien were ground attacks on OB's. A ground attack occurred against the 402nd RF Company OB 8 kilometers NW of Cai Lay in Dinh Tuong Province.

I now had an efficiency sample. Over a nine day period with three days separating each action there had been a total of 353 operations with 21 A&B level VCI killed, 35 captured, and 24 ralliers (usually just a passive activity and not one brought on by search and destroy operations.) What were the unproductive operations doing, going out and camping and drinking? Actually that was a harsh judgment on my part, and as I learned operations were not well targeted, but wandering parties looking for action with the enemy in hiding partly from knowing where the units were going in advance. I mentioned this to COL Cramer, but he said it was on the shoulders of the Vietnamese unit commanders and at least an operation was "out there looking." Interestingly after April 11, results began to increase.

April 12 Results: 135 operations that killed 10, captured 24, and had 7 ralliers for a total of 41 neutralizations. G2 Briefing: 34 incidents, 5 ground attacks with 4 in Kien Thien District of Chuong Thien Province. Can Tho Airfield received 1 round 107 mm and Binh Tuy (Tra Moc Air Base) received 3 round of 107 mm. In Kien Hoa, the An Hoa Ferry struck a VC mine resulting in 50% damage to the ferry.

From this sample of incident reports and activity, Chuong Thien Province was the most active. This correlated with the intelligence reports of movements in Chuong Thien from March onwards. I also noted the proximity of mortar attacks on Can Tho, which meant the VCI were not all eliminated from the area around the Regional Headquarters.

An Tri, I Love Thee

An Tri Detention was controversial. An Tri meant a reshaping of the niceties of police procedures that had previously been placed into law under the Phoenix/Phung Hoang Program in which people were to be arrested, detained for a specific maximum period and their cases to be decided by Province Security Councils on the basis of evidence presented against them. This meant something like the American system of justice with due process of law and decisions by judicial authority however constituted.

An Tri changed all that. An Tri was an emergency measure to change sentencing to indefinite detention. I know not how the other Phoenix Advisors felt, but I strongly favored An Tri detention and communicated it alone to Vietnamese leadership in the Phung Hoang Program. I asked to visit a VC compound and was taken to the edge of Can Tho and shown a detention camp with perhaps 5,000 inside the barriers. The detainees were walking around and talking to each other, which I really disliked, because with the high number of certain suspects, the rest were vulnerable to being ganged up on and converted even if they were innocent. I told my host, :Once detained do not expect anyone to reform and rally to the government. It would be better to let them spend the rest of their lives in the compound." He smiled.

As Douglas Valentine reported in his book, The Phoenix Program, the U.S, Embassy (think Ambassador Bunker), wanted to defer discussion on An Tri. One debate centered around marketing the idea of national review of cases of "preventive detention" as a better option than killing suspects. Another debate point was whether the system would be temporary and avoid either the violation of the GVN Constitution, or the Geneva Convention, which to my mind never needed to be applied to the Vietnam War, since it was an insurgency and not a real war. Then Valentine reports:

While the subject of An Tri was being debated in Saigon, IV Corps Commander Truong in Can Tho authorized, on April 21, 1972, a "special" F6 Phung Hoang campaign designed to neutralize the VCI by moving against suspects with only one adverse report on the record. A response to the Easter offensive, the F6 campaign was started in Chau Doc Province on the initiative of the province chief, who was concerned with reports that NVA units were being guided and assisted by the VCI. More than a thousand VCI suspects were quickly rounded up.

Flying as it did in the face of An Tri reforms, F6 was the cause of some concern. "Mission is aware of potential pitfalls in special Phung Hoang campaign and possibilities of adverse publicity if campaign used for mass round-ups of suspects," wrote Ambassador Bunker. [Source: http://www.american-buddha.com/ phoenixprog28.htm Valentine Chapter 28.]

They must have been reading my mind. I was exultant when the Delta decision on An Tri was made and the F6 Program came into effect. Now we had a more effective tool to use against the VCI. Notice the concern with adverse publicity in the Valentine quote. I was more concerned with adverse deaths of the South Vietnamese civilians without it.

Delta F6 First Report From My Notes

My first F6 note from the morning briefing at the DTOC was taken on April 27, 1972 as follows: Kien Hoa collected 38/Kien Phong – 20. I am not sure why the term F6 was used, since the Vietnamese language does not have the letter "f" but uses "ph" to make the "f" sound. Deep 6 is the Army term for put it in the trash.

Captain Pucket was among the first to leave without a replacement. I have a note he left sometime in April and the Phoenix drawdown was starting.

CHAPTER 11

Intelligence Collection:
May- June 1972

Do You Know the Way to F6 and Bin Tay

My notes from the morning DTOC briefings show that there were 3,263 F6 cases in April and May. I was not told their fate. They were just a number. I assumed, in fact hoped, a good share of them were killed.

In my notes of 19 June 1972 I showed 4,074 F6 results since the inception of the program and 811 more since the 1st of June for a total of 4,885. Obviously at a rate of about 30 per day in mid-June the total by the end of June would be over 5,000. F6 was sanctioned in secret by the GVN and accepted by the American Ambassador and his Phoenix Director as likely to reduce the kill ratio though capture and long term detention.

My advice at the time was not sought, nor was I among the last to advise a counterpart in Phung Hoang—as yet, but my advice would have been to increase the execution ratio for anyone reported in the VCI hierarchy above messenger (Commo-liaison type). My philosophy of war has always been don't take prisoners, take control. Prisoners are simply a waste of time, food, manpower, and the ground on which they walk. Get whatever quick intelligence is available if they are captured and then they are expendable as collateral damage.

Delta Dawns

Major General Nguyen Vinh Nghi took command of IV Corps forces in May and was immediately faced on May 18th with the 1st NVA Division attacking into Kien Giang at a point about 12 miles southeast of the strategic village of Ha Tien. The ARVN fought for ten days and were supported by American air strikes. The NVA retreated across the border to Cambodia with several hundred dead. This ARVN success freed up the provinces west of the Ba Sac River and the situation returned to quiet for the time being. Minor harassment of the PF is all that I have in my notes in that area.

These successes did not mean everything was fine elsewhere as activity flared up in various part of the Delta with the apparent goal being to insert enemy forces into the heart of the Delta between Saigon and Can Tho in Dinh Tuong Province, where my good friend Major Coniglio was in charge of advising the Province Phung Hoang Chief in My Tho. While May had the occasional VC incident of attacking an OB by a sniper or a ship convoy on the Ba Sac or Mekong with two or three mortars, activity picked up in Dinh Tuong during June as followed from my briefing notes.

South Korean Interrogations

I never knew if South Korean helicopter intelligence collection methods were consigned to "urban legends" or if they really took place. The favorite tale of special collection methods related to me was to take several captured VC for a helicopter ride. The South Koreans would then start asking questions. If they did not get a response, they would throw the first VC out of the helicopter and make the others watch him twirl down and crash land without a parachute. Then they would ask some more questions. They either got answers to their questions or returned without the VC. There was no question, however, that the Koreans hated taking prisoners and keeping them as much as I did.

Republic of Korea units did not have the same compunctions or methods of dealing with suspected VC as the Americans. Trained in martial arts hand-to-hand combat combined with their natural stealth (Americans are larger and more conspicuous), Korean troops were feared by the NVA and VC to the point that directives were put out as found in captured documents telling their units to avoid the Koreans at all costs. Korean kill ratio was off the charts at 1 Korean killed for every 25 VC or NVA killed (My own calculations from comparing some of the battles) and in actuality may have been higher overall.

As described by a British War Correspondent, Tim Page,

"The Koreans learned a bastardized version of the Vietnamese language, freed themselves of unnecessary interpreters, and discovered a lot of their assigned ARVN translators were deep cover VC. They took them out and executed them. Korean intelligence was hard and new."

"After a rare chopper assault ferrying in two companies (rare because the US could ill afford choppers for their seconded allies), the Tigers flushed out a dozen VC suspects while I was with them. The suspects were wizened old men, too old for military service, probably VC sympathizer farmers. However, the LZ had been hot with sniper rounds. Terrified woman and children were flushed from the corn breaks claiming "no VC", but everywhere we found fighting holes and bunkers.

> As the CO took a couple of suspects aside to get some updated information, the US forward artillery observer and his radioman drifted off. In bad Vietnamese, the captain barked questions at the cringing suspect. I hardly saw his hands move, and the VC was doubled over, a vivid mark on his neck. Still no answer. Next time, I saw the hand move and heard the forearm break. Writhing now, but still not talking, he was led over to kneel on the edge of one of the fighting holes.

> The CO backed up a couple of paces, brought up his M-2 carbine and, with great pantomime, jacked one up the snout and snicked the safety off. At 15 yards he put a burst of automatic fire a millimeter to the side of the VC's head". The Koreans didn't allow Page to photograph the incident. "I slumped off to join the Americans while the VC spilled his story. Minutes later, when I was taking a leak, he was led down the hill by three ROK's. There was a single pistol shot and the troopers plodded back alone. The ROK's did not believe you could reeducate a communist".

[Source: Elite Korean Units During the Vietnam War. (Hist2004). Quotation by Tim Page. Dated -3/28/2004.

Retrieved from the Internet on 2/2/11 from http://www. militaryphotos.net/forums/archive/index.php/t-8704. html]

Korean units were closer to the danger of communism living in proximity across the DMZ from their homes. Their vivid memories of being attacked was a powerful motivator. Being Asian as fighting near their backyard was also a powerful motivator. Furthermore the men sent were elite units of the Korean Army and were sent to give them combat experience and season them for future training exercises.

I liked my chances in a VC confrontation with a Korean LTC as my new roommate.

Delta Special Police: Bin Tay Campaign

A quiet little program as an adjunct to Phoenix/Phung Hoang was the Special Police Campaign in the Delta called Bin Tay. I have not found any information about the Bin Tay Campaign either in the books on Phoenix or on the Internet. The probable reason for this is that Bin Tay was a regional campaign near the end of the Vietnam War.

While the Regional Forces and Popular Forces (RF/PF) were out chasing down VCI leads and setting ambushes, the Special Police in the Delta concentrated on the intelligence coordination efforts of Phoenix/ Phung Hoang to track down VC cadre in their local sectors. The first note I have on the results of the Bin Tay project are dated May 21, 1972. The results were listed as 1,026 VC targeted, 639 taken into custody, and 54 were discovered to be underground VC. The problem with neutralizing the VC by the Special Police was that the Special Police were to be using agent penetration methods and then agent handling methods to gather intelligence inside the VCI and report on future trends, personnel, and activities. An aggressive move to target and neutralize these potential sources degraded further the intelligence collection effort. The Special Police basically took their intelligence assets and burned them, literally.

The next reporting I had on the Bin Tay Campaign is dated June 3, 1972 when after the briefing I was present when Colonel Son was ordered by General Nghi to begin the Binh Tay Campaign again by June 5. I have a note on the Bin Tay Campaign dated June 5 that "Colonel

Son was asked to attempt to raise police results on the weekends. Coordination should exist between sectors and police. Police should go on Dong Khoi operations. Operations need to be conducted into the less secure areas, while maintaining operations in urban areas." [Peterson, Briefing Notes]

Dong Khoi is the renamed Tu Do Street in Saigon, which itself has been renamed. I cannot bring myself to use the replacement name for Saigon. Tu Do (Liberty) was named Catinat prior to 1955. I have no idea why the operations were named Dong Khoi (General Insurrection) under Bin Tay. My hypothesis is that they were urban roundups of suspected VC agents and probably used cordon and search tactics as was done in the markets of Saigon. Tu Do Street was famous, or infamous as the case may be as having the greatest concentration of "girlie" bars and cabarets. The Majestic Hotel, the Continental Palace Hotel, Caravelle Hotel, and Eden Roc were among the establishments lining Tu Do. I am providing this for the sake of those who remember Saigon during the war. Notre-Dame Cathedral was also on Tu Do. The French Quarter, as it was called was the life of the city and Tu Do was the main street. The French Quarter earned the distinction of being called the Paris of the Orient. Now the street is named Dong Khoi for General Insurrection? Not exactly a name made for the tourism market.

My Intelligence and Operations Briefing Notes dated June 10 show that General Nghi stated better results must be obtained from Bin Tay. He told his staff to immediately implement a rewards and promotion program as stimulus for the campaign. Then he made the statement, "From now on all problems will be solved in one week!" [Peterson: Briefing Notes, 10 Jun 72] The last of my notes until two in August were due to the fact Colonel Cramer decided he did not need them if he attended the morning briefings.

Saigon Phoenix Advisor Conference

The week of June 11, I was sent to Saigon for a Phoenix/Phung Hoang Advisor Conference. The statement was made at the conference that there would be no advisors after December 31, 1972. I sent a letter home to my wife to expect me by the end of the year.

CHAPTER 12

Where Have All the Soldiers Gone:
July to Mid-August 1972

Tactical Situation in the Delta

July and August brought a concentration of enemy regiments in northern Dinh Tuong Province. As LT GEN Truong said in his Monograph, "Dinh Tuong Province was about to become the area for a major contest, and perhaps this was the primary goal of his offensive in the Mekong Delta. [Truong, 150] NVA units were also moving to secure positions and tighten control in the Parrot's Beak near the Mekong River ARVN forces cleared out the area after 22 days of fighting, but upon withdrawal, NVA troops filled the void in Cambodia once again to secure their supply lines. The battles went back and forth, but the ARVN division was needed in the Delta to stave off more threats, particularly in the rear in Dinh Tuong. [Truong, 151]

As presented by LT GEN Truong:

Attack in Dinh Tuong

"The enemy took advantage of the void left in Dinh Tuong Province by the 7th ARVN Division, which was then conducting operations in Cambodia. He launched a series of coordinated attacks against three district towns, Sam Giang, Cai Be and Cai Lay during the period from 17 May to 11 July. The attacking forces initially consisted of elements of the Dong Thap 1 and

Z15 Regiments. All of these attacks were driven back by territorial forces with the strong support provided by U.S. tactical air and helicopter gunships. The enemy was finally forced to withdraw into his base area (470) to refit and recover for future actions. His losses had been heavy.

Despite initial setbacks enemy pressure was also mounting at this time on Route QL-4, the vital supply line between the Delta's rice bowl and the nation's capital. Indications were that the enemy was bringing into the area more troops. As a result, IV Corps had to move the 7th Division back into its tactical area of responsibility, leaving behind only one regiment to form a screen along the border. By that time, the 15th Regiment, 9th ARVN Division had accomplished its mission south of An Loc and was released by MR-3 for return to MR-4. It was immediately deployed to Dinh Tuong at the same time as two ranger groups and the Ranger Command of MR-4. To defeat the enemy's effort against Route QL-4 in Dinh Tuong, B-52 strikes were concentrated on enemy bases in the Delta whenever fighting became intense and profitable targets were detected.

In mid August, as the situation in Binh Long Province became stabilized, the 21st Division was returned to MR-4 and reassigned the responsibility for the southern Hau Giang area, its former territory.

Elements of the 9th Division which formerly operated in this area were directed to the Tien Giang area where they concentrated on Dinh Tuong. These redeployments enabled the 7th Division to devote its effort to Kien Tuong Province in the north and the border area. The 44th STZ meanwhile was assigned the responsibility for the area west of the Mekong River and south of the Cambodian border, to include the eastern part of

Kien Phong Province. The 7th Division was assigned a similar area of responsibility east of the Mekong River, to include the entire province of Kien Tuong.

As a result of this influx of ARVN forces in the Tien Giang area, there was an urgent need for IV Corps to provide better command and control. General Nghi therefore established IV Corps Command Forward at Dong Tam Base and placed Brigadier General Nguyen Thanh Hoang, his deputy for operations, in charge. This rather conventional approach to command and control greatly assisted General Nghi. It facilitated the execution of two major tasks that IV Corps had assigned to its subordinate units, namely to maintain contact with the enemy and destroy his units in the Delta, and to interdict his movements of men and supplies from Cambodia into South Vietnam.

During this period of command and control restructuring, the ranger forces and 9th Division, which were occasionally reinforced with the 10th and 12th Regiments, 7th Division, fought many fierce battles in Dinh Tuong Province and in Base Area 470. In early August, the ranger forces under MR-4 Ranger Command fought a major battle in the Hau My area, west-northwest of My Tho, and completely cleared this area of the enemy. This enabled IV Corps to rebuild a system of outposts along the Thap Muoi Canal and reestablish GVN control over this area which had been subverted by the enemy since the beginning of his Easter Offensive. By the end of August, enemy activities in Dinh Tuong Province had been seriously impeded by our quick and aggressive reactions on the ground and continuous pounding from the air by U.S. tactical air and B-52's.

In late August and early September, IV Corps shifted its effort toward the That Son area in Chau Doc

Province where intelligence reports strongly indicated reinfiltration by elements of the 1st NVA Division.

In a quick move, IV Corps brought its forces westward into Chau Doc and across the Cambodian border into an area west of Nui O. At the same time, it moved the 44th STZ Headquarters back to Chi Lang with the mission of engaging the 1st NVA Division, turning over the province of Kien Phong to the 7th ARVN Division."

The Aftermath

"During the month of September, the situation in the Delta remained relatively uneventful. Not until early October did enemy initiated actions resume again at a high level. The enemy's increased effort appeared to have some connection with the cease-fire agreement which was being finalized in Paris. In this effort, the 1st NVA Division sent its two regiments, the 42d and 101D, south into An Giang Province and concurrently west into the Ba Hon Mountain area near the coast in Ha Tien Province. East of the Mekong River, elements of the 207th NVA and the E2 Regiments, which were operating in the area of Kompong Trabek and north of Cai Cai, also infiltrated into Kien Phong Province. South of the Bassac River, the enemy's 18B, 95A, D1 and D2 Regiments simultaneously moved eastward, establishing blocking positions along lines of communication and among populous areas. This fanning out pattern clearly indicated an attempt by the enemy to extend his presence over the Delta, undoubtedly in preparation for a standstill cease- fire. However, by the end of October when the cease-fire agreement failed to materialize, these activities declined significantly.

In late October and early November, the 7th ARVN Division made several contacts with the enemy in Kien

Phong Province During a battle in the Hong Ngu District where the Mekong River crossed the border, elements of the division, in coordination with territorial forces, annihilated one battalion of the 207th NVA Regiment, taking a total of 73 prisoners during eight days of engagement. This turned out to be the largest single group of enemy prisoners ever captured during the war Most of these prisoners were teen agers, ill-fed and ill-equipped, some without weapons or ammunition. They disclosed that they had been abandoned by their leaders who fled when the fighting became tough.

Along the common boundary of Kien Tuong and Kien Phong Provinces, the 10th Regiment, 7th ARVN Division also harvested repeated success during contacts made with infiltrated elements of the E2 Regiment, 5th NVA Division. These victories were achieved with the significant support of U.S. Army Air Cavalry teams. Finally, an enemy scheme to attack Cao Lanh, the provincial capital of Kien Phong, was preempted by the quick deployment of the 11th and 12th Regiments, 7th Division into this area.

Meanwhile, farther west of the Bassac River, ranger forces of the 44th STZ conducted successful operations in Ha Tien Province and the That Son area. During these operations, they captured several supply caches, destroyed enemy installations and inflicted substantial losses to elements of two NVA regiments, the 52d and 101D of the 1st Division. A battalion commander of the 52d NVA Regiment surrendered to the rangers and he disclosed that his battalion had been so severely mauled by our ambushes and airstrikes that only 30 men were left.

In summary, in spite of his multiple efforts and heavy sacrifices during the Easter Offensive, the enemy accomplished very little in the Mekong Delta. Route

83

QL-4, which was one among the enemy's major objectives, remained open throughout his offensive save for brief periods of traffic interruption. He had failed to strangle our vital lifeline; he had also failed to disrupt our pacification effort. No district town, not even the remotest, be it in Kien Hoa, Ca Mau or along the border, ever fell into enemy hands, even temporarily. Despite some ups and downs in the pacification effort, the enemy was unable to achieve any additional gains in population control. And most remarkably, all our lines of communication, roads or waterways, remained trafficable throughout his offensive.

On their part, the ARVN forces of MR-4 had performed remarkably well. They had effectively prevented the enemy from achieving big gains and had finally defeated him soundly, this despite their initial failure to prevent further infiltration. The accomplishments of the 7th and 9th Divisions, the rangers, and the RF and PF in the Mekong Delta, although not as dramatic as the combat exploits achieved in heroic An Loc, proud Kontum or victorious Tri-Thien, certainly did have a decisive impact on the survival of South Vietnam. Our strategists had always emphasized that, "He who won the battles in the Mekong Delta would win the war in South Vietnam" Not only had IV Corps won the battles in the Mekong Delta but it had done this while sharing nearly one half of its forces with MR-3 and MR-l."
[Truong, 151-155]

R&R #1

R&R stands for rest and relaxation (sometimes called recreation or recuperation) and is a military euphemism for having a week to go somewhere away from a war zone and unwind. The Phoenix Program had the extra perk of two R&R's, so the first one I wanted to spend with my wife and the second one was yet to be determined, but would have to be a lot less expensive, although the flights were free. I felt I had to go by July, since everyone was getting ready to leave and I would need to take care of the Delta in their void.

After checking flights and opportunities out of Vietnam, which had become difficult with so many leaving, I managed to reach Hawaii by my birthday of July 8th. My wife and I decided that Hawaii would be perfect. One of the members from our church in Virginia was an FBI agent and said he would arrange for a special suite, the Presidential one, in one of the best hotels in Hawaii for the same cost as a regular room.

I slept most of the way to Hawaii and arrived in a great frame of mind. My wife had been preparing as well and looked great, although some of my perception may have been due to the time away. We went to the hotel to check in and I asked my wife how to identify the room. She said the reservation was made by a Tom Collins. OK, I thought to myself, this must be a false name. My thoughts were immediately confirmed. The desk clerk reported, "You are in Room 69."

The greatest thing I remember, other than being together was driving to the Ala Moana shopping center to eat at the grand opening of a new Japanese restaurant. I read about it in the newspaper and we went there as the first guests at the evening opening. As we went through the cafeteria style line, we noticed a photographer shooting the occasion. He asked the servers of the Kobe Beef and other treats to pile up our plates. We were given a lot of extras in big quantities and took our loaded plates to the table. He came over and asked about how we happened to find the event and about us. I explained I was stationed in Vietnam and we were on a one week vacation. The photographer loved that and ordered large drinks for the table, then flowers appeared from somewhere. He told us we would be in the Sunday Honolulu newspaper and asked for an address to send photos. I ate my entire plateful, but my wife could only eat half. The photographer then asked us to go through the line again to take more shots and again we had a double load of all the delicacies. I was able to eat another plateful, but neither of us could eat hers. The photographer was true to his word and sent both the newspaper article and several photographs of our feast. I have never eaten so much in my life.

We moved first to the Coco Palms on the Island of Kauai for one night and then to the Royal Hawaiian, where we were part of the background for a Lawrence Welk special from Hawaii. The R&R was a pleasant interlude with wonderful memories resulting from the visit to Hawaii.

CPT ROY PETERSON IN VIETNAM

The Tax Collector Cometh

Wilbur Wilson, DEPCORDS MR IV, asked who could put together a Briefing and Written Report on VC tax collection. One of my colleagues recommended that I be tasked with the effort to collect the information. Accordingly, I sent a request to every Province Phoenix/Phung Hoang Advisor to task their districts with collecting the information. The Briefing was to be for the Province Senior Advisors' Conference for July 30, 1972 and I was on the Agenda of the Conference at 0940 to 1000 hours. The topic was phrased as "VC Quarterly Extortion (Taxation) Analysis MR-4. I was the lowest ranking officer presenting at the conference. The rest were Majors and higher. The DEPCORDS hosted the conference.

I received outstanding information from the Province and District Advisors detailing the extortion (tax+) demands of the VC on the local citizenry. VC oppression in fact far outweighed legitimate tax collection by the GVN and had a profound effect on positively improving the pacification effort in the Delta by their demands on the farmers.

Land Reform/Pacification

Major Varallo passed me a pamphlet produced by Richard H. (Dick) Eney, Director, Land Reform Division, CORDS/MR 4 as he listed it and signed it. The title of the self-produced, but copyrighted pamphlet, "Checkup on Charlie," was the work of a mathematician who in essence proved land reform pacification was a success in the Delta using modeling techniques and that land reform was not linked to original VC demands that land be redistributed.

As the author states in his ABSTRACT, "It is sometimes alleged that the Land to the Tiller (LTTT) Program has been successful only where the Viet Cong controlled the countryside previously and imposed their own 'Land Reform' program. This story has surfaced in news reports and briefings. It's valued to hostile elements in minimizing friendly accomplishment and/or glorifying the Viet Cong 'revolution' is evident." [Eney]

Without presenting six tables of information related to the analysis, in the discussion page (unnumbered) the author says, "The preceding six tables indicate pretyy clearly that there is no correlation between former VC control and Land Reform success. The story that Land to the Tiller is merely a sort of rubber stamping of the Viet Cong 'revolution' is fiction." [Eney]

Land tenancy and ownership in fact was a key factor in pacifying the Delta and degrading VC influence over time. Land redistribution produced a population willing to work with the GVN and the Phoenix program both to separate themselves from the Viet Cong and to attempt to get out from VC extortion (taxation) demands. Self-interest and a stake in the system is essential in any civil administration program success and land reform was no exception.

Thoughts on the War in a Letter to My Wife

The following sentiments are extracted as one whole paragraph from a letter I wrote to my wife on July 31, 1972:

> "There is so much more to this country than the war
> which constantly disturbs the lives of these people. Back
> in the states everyone now seems to think that the war

will go away if we simply pull out and the only reason for staying for the majority has now become the POW issue. There are so many more reasons why we should stay and see the entire problem through. It is funny that our reasons for withdrawal should be as tenuous as our reasons for entering the conflict....

After a while, one really begins to understand these people and respects them despite their weaknesses and faults as in no small sense a people upon whom the tides of history have thrust a battle of larger dimensions. They do not need to realize the larger dimension because they are having enough problems with the here and now.

The North Vietnamese must not be allowed to subject these people who have stood up to superior manpower, who have suffered to get this far so that they could determine their own destiny, and who will be massively murdered when a cease fire comes. And should the (North) Vietnamese succeed in conquering them, beating the breath out of the last supporter of Vietnam Cong-Hoa (Republic), then our shame in getting out should be as great as our embarrassment while we helped." [Peterson, Letter]

Sunday Downtime

Sundays were normally a very peaceful time in Can Tho. On the compound on which we were quartered, steak and chicken dinners were served. I counted my blessings, since I doubted if the Province and District Advisors had such good food and I knew for certain the U.S. Military operating in places like Kontum and An Loc where they were under siege had the opportunity to have a mess hall prepare their meals. Sundays were usually for playing volleyball, water polo, tennis, or handball. After the physical exertion and meal I would often take a nap in my top bunk in the tiny room.

One Sunday as I was sleeping I was alarmingly awakened when a very large rat and nest of baby rats fell through the ceiling on top of me.

My Korean LTC roommate who replaced Captain Little in mid-August was not there, or the rat probably would have been barbequed. I threw the rat against the wall stunning it and then killed it with something, I do not remember what and then stomped out the babies.

Another Sunday (Sundays were the only time I was in the compound during the day) a couple of rounds were lobbed into the area of the compound. One of the Majors came running down the sidewalk and told everyone to put on helmets and get into the bunkers between the buildings. I had never been inside the bunker and did not want to be there, so I said I will make sure the compound is guarded from an attack and headed for a watchtower. After 10 minutes of silence, everyone came out of the bunkers. I had nothing to report and the rest of the day everyone was a little on edge.

Move to the Hotel

After the incident with the rat falling on me, I decided by the end of August I would find a way to move to the small hotel nearby where the previous Phoenix Advisors had stayed and were now vacating. My roommate Captain Ralph Little was gone to Tri Ton District. Now I had a Korean LTC move into my room. I put in the paperwork for the move citing operational considerations and it was approved by the Eakin compound Commander. The only stipulation was that I perform night duty on the duty roster at the compound. I decided that was a fair exchange.

I am not talking about a sumptuous hotel by any stretch of the imagination, but I am talking about my own toilet, shower, table, and bed. I brought along the refrigerator Captain Little and I had purchased, probably from the PX and a small stove. By September I had my own Jeep like vehicle made in Japan and painted yellow green. The bottom floor of the hotel had parking spaces for four vehicles and mine was usually the only one there.

The middle of August brought all the changes and increased work load as anticipated. My letter home dated August 11, 1972 provided some of the details of the changes and increased work:

> "In another week or so, I will probably be flying around
> the Delta more often because I will be making the

89

inspections trips which Ralph (Captain Little) used to do. These trips are usually on Tuesdays and Thursdays. Then there is the matter of writing yup the reports on my return. Now they also want a special two day set of classes for combat arms officers who were not trained in Phung Hoang, but who are now occupying Phung Hoang slots in the provinces and districts. Guess who will make up the program of instruction and who will wind up with the duty of teaching all the material, you guessed it, because there is no one else here who can do this anyway. There is always something I guess—even when a program is going to be gone at the end of the year. I also expect our new Colonel to feel that he must make some positive achievements, although he will only be commanding the Phung Hoang Division for another five months."

"I am now driving a different Jeep which has also solely been assigned to my care. I signed for the Jeep, so that makes me responsible for it in case of theft or damage, etc. At least it starts every morning, which is more than I could say for the previous Jeep. [Peterson, Letter]

CHAPTER 13

Alone and Loving It
August 1972

Well I was not completely alone yet, but I was getting there.

Farewells

August and September brought departures and no replacements, except one. By August 15, Colonel Cramer, Major Donald Palmer, and Captain Max Puckett left and now it was Major Varallo, Captain Little, Captain Whitney, and me with Captain Little headed out shortly to Tri Ton District, Chau Doc Province and Major Varallo to leave in September or early October. Captain Whitney had an original date of November to depart, but was reassigned early. Captain Little was now the Operations Officer, but wanted to complete his tour in a Province on the Cambodian border and receive his Combat Infantryman Badge (CIB).

Colonel Cool

Colonel "Cool" was perhaps the most interesting personality I met in the entire military. I am purposely not providing his name, since the character was so bizarre, so I am using a false name. Prior to his arrival I was called from Saigon and told to" take care" of the Colonel, since he had no Phoenix training. I was also told that he had a head injury that limited him and impaired his speech patterns.

"Taking care" took on a new meaning for me with Colonel Cool.

He really was a kind person to me and I was privileged to work for him. He paid for restaurant meals, got rid of extra reports, and gave me a high efficiency report. I drove him to and from work and to meetings.

Day 1 with Colonel Cool was a revelation. Major Varallo was the first to greet him and introduced Ralph and I along with SGT McClung. When he shown into the office vacated by Colonel Cramer, SGT McClung went in for a couple of minutes and came back out red faced and walked into our main office with a silly grin.

Major Varallo, who loved to imitate people, asked, "What happened? You were not in there very long.

SGT McClung said, "The Colonel asked me to shut the blinds, turn off the lights, and leave.

Major Varallo had already picked up on the strange way of talking of Colonel Cool. "Waall he must need his sleep."

At the prodding of Major Varallo, I went in to see Colonel Cool in the dark to ask if he wanted a briefing.

"No, thank you, son. I am just going to read the most recent information on the program here."

"Shall I turn on the light, Sir, so you can read better?"

"No, thanks, son. I can see well enough."

After a half hour or so, he called across the hall from his office, "Come on over, Captain Peterson."

I dutifully responded and joined him across the hall in the dark. As I wrote In a letter home dated August 18, 1972, I told my wife the substance of the conversation: "Our new COL is understanding of the situation of our program here and is further interested in phasing out the office workload. In fact he suggested that we get a bridge table and have the rest of us sit around and play bridge for the last two or three months."

If Captain Little had any reservations about his decision to go from MR-4 Region HQ to Tri Ton District in Chau Doc Province, I believe his meeting the new Colonel propelled him out the door.

Colonel Cool had been injured in the head when an artillery shell exploded too close to him and he was sent for months of recuperation at the medical facilities in Hawaii. The doctors installed a metal plate in his head and his optical nerves were severely damaged, and perhaps other parts of his brain as well. I figured Saigon did not want him near any decision making desks and sent him down to the Delta for me to monitor.

On August 30 I flew to Tri Ton to Ralph Little and bring him some items he wanted as part of an inspection visit. The Helicopter flew at a more normal altitude of around 2,000 feet as we crossed the rice paddies toward the Cambodian border. Landing in Tri Ton we went through the inspection with my Vietnamese counterpart doing a nice job of checking on the activity and VC counts and then helping coordinate intelligence patterns as we had taught him.

Ralph asked if I would like to go see the border with Cambodia. I said I would so we climbed in his Jeep and headed the short distance to the border. At the border I took a picture and was surprised to see a black pajamed Vietnamese run across the road and dive into the underbrush. We both pulled our .45's, but the man had already disappeared into some tall grass on the Vietnamese side of the border.

We walked up to the border and Ralph said, "Let's go across into Cambodia."

I jokingly replied, "I don't have a visa stamp in my passport for that. In fact I don't have my passport."

We stepped across the border and walked a few steps, just in time to intercept a group of about 20 walking single file from the south to the north. At the head of the column was Co Anh, who had left the CORDS Club a few months before. We called her Annie.

"Annie, what are you doing here in Cambodia," I asked.

"Yeah, Annie. What are they carrying?" asked Ralph.

"They are from my village and we are taking the rice to market" said Annie.

We checked for any weapons and there were none, so we let them proceed with a wave. They looked indeed like they were carrying basked of rice mounted on poles across their shoulders. They had set them down as if unconcerned and rested while we talked with Annie.

Whoever was counting the Americans in Cambodia that day could have added two more, but they never knew. We suspected the column of rice bearers might have been going to feed the VC or NVA, since they were certainly headed in the right direction, but there were some Cambodian villages ahead. We had no reason to detain them, but I have always personally wondered what was going on with Annie and who they really were. They all were shorter than Annie, so they were likely Cambodians and not NVA.

I did take some nice pictures of the only mountains in the Delta Region and figured they were packed with NVA and VC. I told Ralph goodbye and that I would take care of his things left in the room for him and have them sent with his orders as hold baggage when he leaves.

Meanwhile back at the Phoenix office, according to my letter of September 10, Colonel Cool walked into the closet in the operations room thinking it was the doorway out. He insisted on wearing nothing but civilian clothes not only around the Delta, but on frequent trips to Saigon, probably to a clinic. To hear me he had to put on his glasses which contained a hearing aid. No one could understand his jokes and they all fell flat. He must have been saving a lot of electricity, since he never allowed the lights in his office to be turned on.

Colonel Cool's next trick was to write a letter to the DEPCORDS requesting closure of the Phoenix office by October and assigning me to the National Police as an Advisor until an adjusted DEROS (departure) date of December 20th. DEPCORDS did not accept the proposal, but apparently COL Cool knew people to talk to in Saigon where he spent most of his time anyway leaving Major Varallo and myself to do as we pleased. I remained a Phoenix Advisor until the end of November, although on November 1, I was reassigned for command and control purposes with no one left but me. DEPCORDS also did not reduce reporting requirements.

According to my letter home dated September 17th, Colonel Cool was taking me everywhere as his spokesman on all subjects related to intelligence collection methods, VC status in the Provinces, economic data on pacification, reporting on VC extortion and taxes, and a host of other issues. For example, I wrote, "Yesterday (September 16) I met with the US Councilor for Economic Affairs who came down from Saigon to listen to economic problems of the Delta. Since I wrote the last VC Extortion Study in July, the COL takes me around as his expert on this subject and I consequently sit in on some interesting meetings. The main problem yesterday seemed to be a rice policy debate and a tax policy problem on which level of Vietnamese government should do what.

The work I was now doing on reports sent in from all the Provinces and Districts as well as prescribed reports to Saigon had formerly been performed by six people, so one can appreciate the workload and time spent in the office. If there were any VC in Can Tho, they could have targeted my vehicle and me for elimination after midnight on the way back to the hotel where I now was staying. I had to stay at the hotel, because the gates closed at Eakin compound anyway by 2200 hours as a safety measure.

CHAPTER 14

Guns Along the Bassac
August and September 1972

Delta Inspection Visits

From a letter I wrote on September 19th to my wife I have been able to reconstruct my inspection visits in the Delta from August 16th to September 18th. They are as follows:

August 16 (Wednesday), Huong My District, Kien Hoa Province

I noted that I flew to Huong My District in Kien Hoa Province and visited with Dennis Deeny from the MASA course we were in together. Huong My is and active VC area in a province "that has a plentiful supply of VC." I did not put it in the letter, but our helicopter took fire from an area pocked marked by an Arc Light strike by B52's. I was told I could get the air medal for taking fire, but I thought the medal should be reserved for those who flew a lot and not sporadically like I did.

August 21 (Monday), Vinh Chau District, Bac Lieu Province

I thought the village was in a pleasant location close to the China Sea, but it was an infiltration point from the sea for VC supplies coming into the Delta and must have had some VC well positioned to be able to avoid patrols. Although there was only silt and salt and no sand, I still liked the area. I took a picture of a Buddhist Temple in a jungle setting as we flew close over the top.

August 22 (Wednesday), Cho Gao District, Dinh Tuong Province

I met Major Coniglio from Province at Cho Gao and he had recovered nicely from being shot in July. He told me he had already received his next assignment and it was to West Point as an Instructor in Latin American Affairs.

August 30 (Wednesday), Tri Ton District, Chau Doc Province

I already mentioned this visit, but made another note in this letter that Captain Ralph Little was enjoying being out on his own away from Can Tho, and presumably the Colonel.

September 4 (Monday), Thot Not District, An Giang Province

I drove to Thot Not with my Jeep alone. Thot Not was probably one of the most pacified districts in the entire Delta because of the strong Hoa Hao presence. From my notes in my letter dinner consisted of raw fish, eel, steamed turtle, grass salad, and mint leaves. That was topped off with a dessert of hot water, sugar, and leaves from a bush that tasted a little like elm leaves.

September 11 (Monday), My An District, Kien Phong Province

I flew to My An in the dangerous tri-border area with Kien Tuong, Dinh Tuong, and Kien Phong. The location was a physical wreck. The U.S. Advisors were out on operations with the National Police. I had sufficient language experience to conduct the inspection alone and report back on the results.

September 12 (Tuesday), Ke Sach District, Ba Xuyen Province

I drove with the inspection team to two villages in Ke Sach District, Ba Xuyen Province and was invited to another "feast" after the inspection. This one consisted of seaweed soup, blood sausage, fried turnips, and rice with nuoc mam (the fish sauce).

September 15 (Friday), Lich Hoi Trung District, Ba Xuyen Province

We flew to Soc Trang and picked up the Province Advisor, Preston Funkhaouser and then flew to Lich Hoi Trung, which was a lot like Vonh Chau and close to the South China Sea. This was another area of infiltration into the Delta from the sea for VC/NVA supplies.

September 18 (Monday), Minh Duc District, Vinh Long Province

We flew first to Vinh Long City to pick up major Anderson, the Province Advisor and found Minh Duc to be a highly pacified district in a sea of VC. The District is bordered by the mouth of the Mekong River and is a key location to observe boats of the VC trying to infiltrate the Delta. I noted the rice harvest looked good for November.

Free Steak Nights

Eakin compound began providing free steak nights every week. From a letter I wrote on September 24th, the reasons are explained:

"Last night I enjoyed another free steak dinner. Every week for the last three weeks there has been free steak night with choice T-bones and New York strips. They are the best steaks that I have eaten in Vietnam. This is paid for by an excess in the unit fund, left from those who have been stationed here before. The way it works is that an organization receives so much money for each person who belongs to it from Army resources such as PACEX and PXs. If unspent, this money can accumulate rather rapidly and that is the case here. They have a tiotal of around $30,000 to spend on such projects for the less than 200 men that now remain in our compound."

Shot at by River

On an inspection visit to Vinh Long Province as I was talking to Major Anderson, a radio call came in to the PIOCC that the District across the Bassac was being attacked in the daytime by VC. On this particular trip, my Vietnamese counterpart had procured the boat for the visit. Since we were all told the new simultaneously, I asked by counterpart what he wanted to do.

His answer was, "We will go across the river and reinforce the defenders."

"Great, I said. Let's go, I responded."

I was thinking this may be as close to the action other than being shot at on occasion that I would ever get on this tour. We ran down to the boat and quickly embarked. As we headed across the river several shots sounded, but we did not hear the bullets. The boat pilot had apparently been under fire before and he began a zig zag course directly for the opposite shore where there were tall reeds. Tucking up close to the bank and reeds on the other side provided cover as he headed down river to the District. Approaching the District town, we saw two dead bodies of possible VC floating in the water next to the shore.

We got out of the boat and found the District Phoenix Advisor with the District Military Advisor standing outside their compound with weapons drawn. Some fire was heard not far away, but they said everything was reported by their Vietnam defenders at the outposts to be under control and the attack was beaten back, or else the attackers had simply wanted to make a show of power by firing on the District compound. Either way we stayed until the firing subsided and then departed for Can Tho.

This visit completed my trifecta. I had now been shot at by driving in the Delta, by flying in helicopters (twice), and while boating down the Bassac.

CHAPTER 15

Advice Above and Beyond
October 1972

October 1972 and I was one of 125 Phoenix Advisors left in Vietnam. I was flying under the radar, but that was about to change internally with program insiders. Major Varallo was my boss until near the end of the month, but I was turned loose to conduct Phoenix business as I saw fit. Colonel Cool cared less and as I said spent a lot of time traveling to Saigon anyway. Operations were left up to me. What was not realized was that by now I had earned a great deal of respect from the Vietnamese for speaking their language and interpreting for them and for a more direct role in intelligence collection and analysis, especially working on pattern analysis that Major Phenniger, the Sa Dec Phoenix Advisor had presented at one of the conferences in Can Tho. I spent all my time on inspection visits all over the Delta, writing reports, and working in the RIOCC, as I liked to call it, though such a name was never given for a Regional Intelligence Operations and Command Center. I thought it should have been called that, since it functioned like a super PIOCC and DIOCC.

My thought was since the VC had alternative boundary markers and names for the Provinces and Districts the only place to really ensure a coordinated intelligence collection and analysis effort, prepare the proper targeting using the right techniques, and then assassinating the VC was from above at MR-4 level. The programs I advised about, taught to the Vietnamese, and monitored were outside the scope of normal duties, but not outside the scope of winning a war. What I did was not a matter of record and essentially I was unsupervised except to find out where I was at supper and breakfast.

My schedule was sent home in a letter dated October 13th:

"My daily routine goes like this: Get up in the morning at 0600, eat breakfast at 0700, be at work by 0800, brief in the morning (DEPCORDS) between 0800 and 0900, work on reports until 1200, eat and relax between 1200 and 1400, work on reports until 1800, eat (at the CORDS Club) from 1800 to 1900, and then return to the office to work until midnight.

The schedule was deceptive, since both morning and afternoon hours were spent either on inspections or working with my counterpart in the Phung Hoang office. The evenings were the real report writing time.

My schedule was about to change again as I wrote in a letter dated October 19th:

"It appears that the (American) Phung Hoang Division is disintegrating. Two days ago COL (Cool) was provided with another job in Saigon and he leaves tomorrow on 20 October to take over that assignment. At the same time, the Deputy Phung Hoang Advisor (Major Varallo) is leaving this weekend to DEROS and then go to Germany. That leaves we three Captains and one NCO. We are now being downgraded from a Division status at CORDS to work under the auspices of another Division called Plans, Programs, and Reports (PP&R). The physical move will be made on 1 November..."

My October 22nd letter shows that I had written a 30 page Quarterly Report on VC Extortion. Since I completed it a week ahead of time, DEPCORDS found out I had a first draft and was personally called to go over the report on Sunday afternoon. He liked the in depth report so much in first draft form he took it and said he wanted to send it in now and not wait, but to go back and keep working for the final report and personal briefing, which was to be given to the Quarterly Province Security Advisor Conference set for the next Sunday. I did have the carbon copy of the report and had to go back and retype it while editing it for the Conference distribution. Later I learned from one of my sources that one of my CIA cohorts got a copy of the report and turned it in as their own and the person that did so received a promotion.

Terminate With Extreme Prejudice

By the end of October, after working directly with my Phung Hoang counterpart and those that worked for him, we had made a lot of training and targeting advances and molding an effective and efficient quiet campaign for terminating all VC with extreme prejudice.

Major Thieu was obviously worried. As I walked into the Phung Hoang office of the Vietnamese, I could smell the scent of the dark red bougainvillea through the open windows, the ones without any glass and the covers pushed up to let in the pleasant morning breezes. Major Thieu and I began discussing options for the Phung Hoang effort. I told Major Thieu that the Americans were continuing to leave and that I did not know how long there would be advisors.

Major Thieu said, "I have reports that the 1ˢᵗ North Vietnamese Division is moving farther to the south than usual and that they may try to come in from Cambodia through Kein Giang, and Chau Duc Provinces. What can we do?"

"I have a plan for you, but it will take a lot of men to do it," I responded. "The newly converted PF into the RF are perfect for you to employ effectively besides the PRU and National Police.

"Please advise me," he asked.

I laid out a verbal ten point plan for him in simple Vietnamese. I put nothing in writing so no one could blame anyone. Here are the ten points I had in my mind and attempted to communicate:

1. Order the apprehension of all suspects, even if on a one time charge by someone, and even if low level Commo-liaison types. (Same as An Tri Detentions and the F6 Program begun in the Delta.)
2. Set curfews. Anyone out after 10 pm is considered a suspect. Shoot them on the spot or detain them in the camps.
3. Suspend processing through the Phoenix Councils. (Same as An Tri Detentions and the F6 Program begun in the Delta.)
4. Place everyone collected in long term detention camps. Build more and expand them if you have to do so. (Same as An Tri Detentions and the F6 Program begun in the Delta.)
5. Move all permanent blocking positions to new ones and then alternate locations.

6. Do not announce any raids or movements in advance. Do so only at the briefing for departure.
7. Execute the guilty on charges. Expand the meaning of guilty to anyone helping the communists.
8. Shoot anyone coming from Cambodia or along the border in Cambodia.
9. Take some of the Hoa Hao from An Giang and use them in Kien Giang Province.
10. Take away the food supply of rice from all suspected VC controlled hamlets and leave them just enough for a family to eat for three days. Make them go to a government controlled hamlet or village to get more. Pay them for what was taken. In this way they cannot feed the VC or NVA coming into the Delta.

I did not know it, but my advice at the beginning of October was about to be supported by the Government of Vietnam and signed into a Decree Law five days before my departure from the Delta on November 30. I take no credit for the Decree Law, since the exigencies of the political situation left no choice for the President of Vietnam and his core of Phung Hoang Advisors. President Thieu clearly saw the same situation I did concerning points 1, 3, and 4. The An Tri detention program and the F6 program instituted back in May 1972 in which even one report was sufficient rather than three to incarcerate or attack presumed VCI made a major difference in the Delta. These were reinforced by the secretive Delta only (as far as I knew) Bin Tay Program.

Douglas Valentine provides a cogent presentation of the events of October and November 1972 surrounding what I call the revitalization of Phoenix/Phung Hoang:

> [I]n October 1972, a tentative agreement was reached calling for the formation of a National Council for Reconciliation and Concord composed of representatives from the GVN, NLF, and Third Force neutralists. On October 24, President Thieu presented sixty-nine amendments to the agreement and, stating that the VCI "must be wiped out quickly and mercilessly," ordered

a new wave of arrests. On November 25, 1972, three weeks after Richard Nixon was reelected, Thieu signed Decree Law 020, "Concerning National Security and Public Order." Issued in secret, 020 modified An Tri to the extent, Ambassador Bunker wrote, "that these powers are no longer limited to wartime and may be applied following a ceasefire and the end of an officially declared state of war. The evident purpose of the law is to provide for an extension of An Tri procedures in preparation for a ceasefire confrontation with the Communists."

Broadening An Tri to include people deemed dangerous to "public order," Bunker wrote, "means that virtually any person arrested in South Vietnam can now be held on criminal instead of political charges."

The "public order" provision was included in Decree Law 020 precisely because the cease-fire agreement prohibited the incarceration of political prisoners. According to Decree Law 020, Communist offenders already in jail under the An Tri Laws would also have their sentences automatically extended. Likewise, Province Security Committees were directed to extend automatically the detention of categories A and B VCI until the end of the "present emergency," which did not end with the cease-fire.

As a result of Decree Law 020, thousands of Vietnamese remained incarcerated until April 1975. On December 18, 1972, Newsweek estimated that there were forty-five thousand "official" prisoners in Vietnamese prisons and another hundred thousand in detention camps. Amnesty International reported at least two hundred thousand political prisoners, and other observers cited higher estimates. The U .S. Embassy identified on its computer tapes fewer than ten thousand political

prisoners and called the criticism unfounded in light of An Tri reforms.
[Source: Douglas Valentine. The Phoenix Program. Chapter 28. Pages 401-402]

1. Apprehensions

The key to all my advice was removal of all discernible possibilities for assistance to infiltrating or exfiltrating NVA was cutting the lines of communication and eliminating anyone who might help them find their way over the terrain in their Province and Area of Operations. The concept is like weeding a garden. Kill the weeds and remove the seeds. In this case the idea was to weed the pacification garden and allow the good grass to grow to fill in the void. This matched the objectives of the An Tri and F6 programs begun and implemented in the Delta and was no more than a statement by me to my counterpart to continue programs already legitimized in the South.

2. Curfews

Curfews were often used and sometimes enforced. The central point of talking about curfews was to kill anyone out past the curfew time and not just apprehend them. That was my advice.

3. Suspend Processing

Processing for judicial review by the Province Security Councils was already pretty much a foregone conclusion, since An Tri Detention did the same thing.

4. Long Term Detention

Long term detention meant anyone incarcerated would be held until the national state of emergency was over. As discussed by Valentine earlier, the emergency lasted until the North Vietnamese invasion in 1975. I was gratified to discover that between the 145,000 in prison and detention camps and the Amnesty International estimate of 200,000 still incarcerated in 1975, the GVN agreed with my advice, or perhaps as the case may be, my advice correlated with the GVN choices.

5. Move all Permanent Blocking Positions to New Locations

This was logical advice. Many of the Observation Bases and Posts had remained the same over the course of the war. Now was the time to begin playing a shell game and made the VC start guessing, rather than knowing the locations of ambushes, traps, and posts. The old locations could still be used or lightly defended with reinforcements within easy reach of them from either the new location or from resources for reaction to be added behind both for easy movement to reinforce.

6. Do Not Announce Movements to Alternate Positions or for Raids and Ambushes in Advance

The usual method of operations was advance announcement of where all the forces were going to be at a given time in advance of their getting there. That meant any low level VC operating from a National Police station or even from a nightclub could communicate on how to avoid or attack local forces for the PRU, PSDF, and other police and paramilitary assets. This had to change so that now the grimy little VC fish could get fried.

7. Execute the Guilty

I made a strong pitch to my counterpart that the guilty were just a drain on resources including food and manpower to watch them. Immediate executions were more efficient and freed up needed resources. Only two pieces of evidence were sufficient and not three and if founded on a document of VCI names only one was sufficient. For example one could be accused in a hamlet or village and corroborated by another witness. That would be sufficient to execute. I also recommended that in the event of an NVA attack, all detainees should be executed. This apparently did not happen, or I would have reduced the prisoner and detention count by at least half in 1975 by eliminating all prisons and camps in the Delta.

8. Shoot Anything Coming Through Cambodia

If anyone coming across the Cambodian border could not identify themselves as ARVN, PRU, or other official unit, shoot them.

9. Use the Hoa Hao

The Hoa Hao in Chau Doc, An Giang, and Sa Dec were all virulent anti-communists as I had learned and admired from the time the Communists executed their Buddhist leader. These Buddhists were not pacifists, but were aggressive in defense of their religion. They could be further used in Observation Posts and ambushes in Kien Giang the southernmost entrance from Cambodia and an adjacent province to the south of both Chau Doc and An Giang and in Kien Phong to the north.

10. Reduce Food Supply

I am not sure that I got through on the point of taking away the food supply that could be used to feed the VC and NVA infiltrators. The idea was based on Maslow's Hierarchy of Needs that food was critical to survival and on his pyramid occupied the top of the triangle of human needs as one of the physiological requirements. By reducing the food supply and making inhabitants dependent on the government by repurchasing rice and other necessities from government agencies, the VC and NVA would have greater difficulty in obtaining food without killing entire hamlets and villages and even then they would get limited rations.

The population would be focused on feeding family and not the enemy. If the VC or NVA thought they could get food from the government agents, they would have to expose themselves repeatedly, since food supply would be limited to a family to three days and they could only purchase enough to feed their size of registered family with all names included along with ages.

COL Kelleher and the Call

Sometime in late October I was summoned to the manpower depleted CORDS Headquarters for a phone call from Col Kelleher from the

Phoenix Office in Saigon. The line was bad and it was difficult to hear him, but I believe I understood after several attempts and line outages. The conversation went something like this:

"Captain Peterson, what are you doing in the Delta?"

"Well sir, I am advising my Phung Hoang counterpart on what to do now and when I leave Vietnam."

"I have heard stories about you from our Province advisors and they seem disturbed."

"I cannot imagine why, Sir."

"There are reports of large scale apprehensions and detentions without any cases being brought to the Province Councils."

"Oh, that's interesting, Sir, but you knew about the An Tri and F6 Campaigns in which the GVN authorized apprehensions and detentions without opening cases or bringing them to the Province Councils for disposition."

Colonel Keliher responded, "I am emphasizing the large scale of apprehensions and detentions coupled with a much higher rate of VCI being killed"

"I guess the National and Special Police along with the restructuring and conversion of the PF into the RF as commanded by General Nghi in the Delta must have had a positive effect on the numbers of detainees and kills. Would you like to hear about Bin Tay?"

"Is that a District?"

"No, Sir, It is another new program of cordon and search in the Delta by restructured forces."

"OK, Send me a report. Just between us you are doing an amazing job."

"Thank you, sir. Why do you say that?"

"Apparently you somehow have blunted a major North Vietnamese incursion and are responsible for killing at least 4,000 NVA trying to enter the Delta. As I hear it, there are no Commo-liaison guides to get them past the blocking positions and traps. They are running directly into kill zones from new positions and then try to end run past the old ones and there are units there to kill them as well. Personally I believe it is great, but some of the higher ups are questioning the legality of what is happening in the Delta."

"Well, Sir, as you know I am only an advisor and am just trying to do the best I can do to help my counterpart. I provide advice and the

Vietnamese either use it or lose it. We Americans are on the sidelines and whatever the Vietnamese do is their business."

"I hear you. Good luck."

"Thank you, Sir."

I have always privately been satisfied that my advice may have killed 4,000 or more NVA and VC from October to November and if the effort continued, for a long time and for a lot more kills not to mention thousands of incarcerations.

Have I left out a lot of secrets about what I did and advised? Yes, but that story will never be told.

No remorse. Just satisfaction. The Delta was stable.

CHAPTER 16

Goodbye Vietnam
November 1972

November and I was really on my own. I was assigned to PP&R, but did not spend much time there. After all, there was no place to get lunch by their offices. The CORDS Club was still open and close by the office, so why leave. As for PP&R, they did not know what to do with me anyway. I saw my main function as securing the last of the helicopters for inspection visits for the Vietnamese Phung Hoang Team and especially for my counterpart and began a round of tours of the Delta Region without finding many American Advisors left.

The other function was continuing to work on intelligence collection methods and how to handle agents in the field. The Bin Tay Program had taken down a lot of structures and agents had to be removed for their safety and resettled elsewhere.

Yellow Alert

"Yellow Alert! "MR-4 can't call one just before I go home," I said to some Sergeant on Eakin Compound. "I have work to complete at the office and now they don't want me to leave this stupid compound and go to the office."

"Well, Captain, the G2 just called the alert. He must have a good reason."

"I am not so sure about that, Sarge. I think it may be just because there are so few of us left and he wants us to stay in one place and not have us wandering around."

I headed for the compound office. "Lieutenant Colonel Jackson (a replacement name), I request permission to leave the compound."

"What for, my young about to be pounced on Captain?"

"Sir, I still have a tremendous quantity of work to complete for the briefing on VC Financing of the War in the South as Extortion. You can just imagine how the special Ambassador to Vietnam, Mr. Colby would like to wait on such a fine report, especially when he requested I personally prepare one like the previous one I prepared and sent him. Besides he is sending Mr. Tilton from Phoenix down here for the briefing and to pick up the report."

Lieutenant Colonel Jackson regarded me with suspicion and then said, "Man, that sounds like something they ought to be doing at the Combined Document Research Center in Saigon, or back in the states, not here in the Delta. What are you doing anyway on such a far-fetched topic?"

The MR-4 Cords Director wants us to do it, probably to keep credit here for the work that is collected and prepared in a written report. The report is only about the Delta, anyway. The topic is a vital one for understanding VCI and NVA operations and is not far-fetched. Here is my Special Operations Pass that allows me the right to go anywhere at any time in the Delta. I have a mission to complete and it is only a few blocks to the office. Do we have an understanding?"

Lieutenant Colonel Jackson bowed to the logic, the pressure of superior officers, a mission oriented approach and to my free access and egress pass. "Get gone now, but don't get blown up or shot. I do not want to have to answer for you. I have better things to do than stand here and argue with you all night. Make sure you sign out on the register."

"Yes sir," I grinned as I moved quickly out the door to my waiting Jeep. Leaving the compound I showed my pass to the American sentry at the gate, who had no more clue about the meaning of the free movement pass than the Lieutenant Colonel, but the words and the official looking document were sufficient to allow me to leave the compound and head for a midnight of work and then back to the hotel for the rest of the night.

"How are you doing, tonight, Sergeant," I asked as I slowly rolled up to him at the gate.

The sentry nervously replied, "I am a little spooked by the Yellow Alert and with the Ruff/Puff whistling and singing all night."

"Why are they doing that?"

Because that lets the VC know where they are so they won't be attacked, responded the Sergeant. "They are just plain scared. The whistling ain't exactly designed to put fear in the hearts of the Viet Cong."

Since I had picked up the duty of working with the Ruff/Puff and the National Police in addition to Phoenix duties, I knew the real reason for the whistling was both to boost morale for themselves and as a form of maintaining contact with the next listening post. The absence of a whistle for too long a period of time was an indicator trouble was on the way.

Last One to Leave Turn Out the Lights

Major Trevor Bissey was assigned to Phoenix in the Delta from someplace else in Vietnam and the two of us worked on reports and inspection visits. I was surprised to have someone come to the Delta for Phoenix, but I believe the DEPCORDS insisted on it. Besides, I was leaving by the end of the month. Trevor went to the PP&R Office and I stayed most of the time at the old Phoenix office or at the Phung Hoang office.

I presume Trevor was the last one to leave and the one who turned out the lights on the Phoenix Program in the Delta. I wanted to be the one, but had orders to leave Vietnam on December 1. That meant leave the Delta on November 30th.

Order of the Delta Dragon

I received the coveted Order of the Delta Dragon, a certificate that meant almost as much to me as the other awards I received. The certificate could not be included in my personnel jacket, but it said I had made a difference.

Helicopter from Hell November 30

As I boarded the Huey for my last flight out of the Delta I saw the pilot and co-pilot who said they were also leaving. They were combat helicopter pilots and I figured with the door gunner at the ready, we would have no problems. I had no idea what kind of flight awaited me as we headed north by northeast.

The pilot told me to really buckle in well, so I pulled it extra tight. As we headed out, we did not pick up altitude but instead were flying at what I judged to be 50 feet or less. We clipped one branch off a tree with the rotors aqs we climbed and continued from there. The terrain with the rice paddies rapidly receded as startled farmers glanced up at our approach and passing. The pilot called back to me and said this was the normal way that all Huey combat pilots flew upon leaving so as not to give any VC a shot. I was thinking the opposite, that the low level flying would make an inviting target. On the other hand as we flew closer to the trees at about 25 feet now off the ground, I understood that we were almost invisible until the sound washed over the ground and no one could tell we were coming. By the time we passed, they were too late. The door gunner fired his guns on a couple of occasions as he saw ground fire from behind the chopper from two different tree lines, one I estimated as over Vinh Long Province and the other Dinh Tuong. I was thinking the Surface-to-Air Missiles (SAMS) the VC had hidden in the Delta could easily shot down the scurrying Huey, but then I could have taken them too long to arm themselves.

A bus was waiting for us and several other arrivals to take us to Camp Alpha. The full circle was closing. There was a lot of exuberance and war stories at the barracks, except for me. I was worried about too many Vietnamese military and civilian friends to rejoice. I felt as if we had left a job almost finished. That is no way to play a game. My high school football coach taught me that.

I thought about what my high school football coach said. As a freshman, I was a running back. The coach put the ball on the 20 yard line and gave us five plays to go the length of the field against the first string defense. Gary George, a large freshman lineman opened up a hole for me on the first play and I outran the defense until I reached the other 20 thinking that was good enough. The coach came running after me and said, "Young man, you finish every run you make as if your tail feathers are on fire, because if you don't I will give you some licks with a paddle. This was Texas football after all. I immediately put on the afterburners and ran through the end zone. That is how we should have finished the war—at the border with China.

December 1, 1972: Goodbye Vietnam

I wanted to remain in Vietnam until January at the time of my original Date of Expected Return from Overseas (DEROS), but I had already been granted an extra month and was among the final 16,000 advisors to leave Vietnam. The Pentagon had announced that American troop withdrawal was completed by November 30, 1972. I wanted to see what the Delta was like in January, but the Pentagon had other objectives in mind and I was to report to the MI Officer Advanced Course at Fort Huachuca, Arizona in January 1973.

My emotions were mixed as I boarded the plane they called the "Freedom Bird." All military flights out of Vietnam were called this. I hated to leave Vietnam to my friends to fend off the communists. I hoped they had the fortitude to continue the fight without American backing and aggressiveness. I trusted the principles I had put in place would continue to serve the Delta well. I wanted someone to drop a "nuc" on Hanoi. I desired to personally kill Viet Cong, but was denied that by Vietnamization. It was time, however, to see my wife and young daughter and rebuild family life.

CHAPTER 17

Final Tally

Honor, as I learned, is an elusive term. Can a retreat from responsibility be honorable? Can supporting a government just a little longer insure its survival? Can an additional two weeks of bombings change Hanoi policy and bring real honor to leaving Vietnam? It took years for me to get answers to questions about honor.

Several sources list the final Phoenix/Phung Hoang Program neutralizations at 81,470.

> "Between 1968 and 1972, Phoenix 'neutralized' 81,740 people suspected of NLF membership, of whom 26,369 were killed. This was a large proportion of the NLF and, between 1969 and 1971, the program was quite successful in destroying NLF infrastructure in many important areas. By 1970, communist plans repeatedly emphasized attacking the government's pacification program and specifically targeted Phoenix officials. The NLF also imposed quotas. In 1970, for example, communist officials near Da Nang in northern South Vietnam instructed their assassins to "kill 400 persons" deemed to be government 'tyrant[s]' and to 'annihilate' anyone involved with the pacification program. Several North Vietnamese officials have made statements about the effectiveness of Phoenix. According to William Colby, 'in the years since the 1975, I have heard several references to North Vietnamese and South Vietnamese

communists who account, who state that in their mind the most, the toughest period that they faced in the whole period of the war from 1960 to 1975 was the period from 1968 to '72 when the Phoenix Program was at work.'"

[http://www.historyplace.com/unitedstates/vietnam/index-1969.html]

APPENDIX I

Vietnam Chronology 1972
[Source: History Place]

Vietnam Chronology 1972

1972

January 25, 1972 - President Nixon announces a proposed eight point peace plan for Vietnam and also reveals that Kissinger has been secretly negotiating with the North Vietnamese. However, Hanoi rejects Nixon's peace overture.

February 21-28 - President Nixon visits China and meets with Mao Zedong and Prime Minister Zhou Enlai to forge new diplomatic relations with the Communist nation. Nixon's visit causes great concern in Hanoi that their wartime ally China might be inclined to agree to an unfavorable settlement of the war to improve Chinese relations with the U.S.

March 10, 1972 - The U.S. 101st Airborne Division is withdrawn from Vietnam.

March 23, 1972 - The U.S. stages a boycott of the Paris peace talks as President Nixon accuses Hanoi of refusing to "negotiate seriously."

March-September - The Eastertide Offensive occurs as 200,000 North Vietnamese soldiers under the command of General Vo Nguyen Giap wage an all-out attempt to conquer South Vietnam. The offensive is a tremendous gamble by Giap and is undertaken as a result of U.S. troop withdrawal, the strength of the anti-war movement in America likely preventing a U.S. retaliatory response, and the poor performance of South Vietnam's Army during Operation Lam Son 719 in 1971.

Giap's immediate strategy involves the capture of Quang Tri in the northern part of South Vietnam, Kontum in the mid section, and An Loc in the south.

North Vietnam's Communist leaders also hope a successful offensive will harm Richard Nixon politically during this presidential election year in America, much as President Lyndon Johnson had suffered as a result of the 1968 Tet Offensive. The Communists believe Nixon's removal would disrupt American aid to South Vietnam.

March 30, 1972 - NVA Eastertide attack on Quang Tri begins.

April 2, 1972 - In response to the Eastertide Offensive, President Nixon authorizes the U.S. 7th Fleet to target NVA troops massed around the Demilitarized Zone with air strikes and naval gunfire.

April 4, 1972 - In a further response to Eastertide, President Nixon authorizes a massive bombing campaign targeting all NVA troops invading South Vietnam along with B-52 air strikes against North Vietnam. "The bastards have never been bombed like they're going to bombed this time," Nixon privately declares.

April 10, 1972 - Heavy B-52 bombardments ranging 145 miles into North Vietnam begin.

April 12, 1972 - NVA Eastertide attack on Kontum begins in central South Vietnam. If the attack succeeds, South Vietnam will effectively be cut in two.

April 15, 1972 - Hanoi and Haiphong harbor are bombed by the U.S.

April 15-20 - Protests against the bombings erupt in America.

April 19, 1972 - NVA Eastertide attack on An Loc begins.

April 27, 1972 - Paris peace talks resume.

April 30, 1972 - U.S. troop levels drop to 69,000.

May 1, 1972 - South Vietnamese abandon Quang Tri City to the NVA.

May 4, 1972 - The U.S. and South Vietnam suspend participation in the Paris peace talks indefinitely. 125 additional U.S. warplanes are ordered to Vietnam.

May 8, 1972 - In response to the ongoing NVA Eastertide Offensive, President Nixon announces Operation Linebacker I, the mining of North Vietnam's harbors along with intensified bombing of roads, bridges, and oil facilities. The announcement brings international condemnation of the U.S. and ignites more anti-war protests in America.

During an air strike conducted by South Vietnamese pilots, Napalm bombs are accidentally dropped on South Vietnamese civilians, including children. Filmed footage and a still photo of a badly burned nude girl fleeing the destruction of her hamlet becomes yet another enduring image of the war.

May 9, 1972 - Operation Linebacker I commences with U.S. jets laying mines in Haiphong harbor.

May 1, 1972 - NVA capture Quang Tri City.

May 15, 1972 - The headquarters for the U.S. Army in Vietnam is decommissioned.

May 17, 1972 - According to U.S. reports, Operation Linebacker I is damaging North Vietnam's ability to supply NVA troops engaged in the Eastertide Offensive.

May 22-30 - President Nixon visits the Soviet Union and meets with Leonid Brezhnev to forge new diplomatic relations with the Communist nation. Nixon's visit causes great concern in Hanoi that their Soviet ally might be inclined to agree to an unfavorable settlement of the war to improve Soviet relations with the U.S.

May 30, 1972 - NVA attack on Kontum is thwarted by South Vietnamese troops, aided by massive U.S. air strikes.

June 1, 1972 - Hanoi admits Operation Linebacker I is causing severe disruptions.

June 9, 1972 - Senior U.S. military advisor John Paul Vann is killed in a helicopter crash near Pleiku. He had been assisting South Vietnamese troops in the defense of Kontum.

June 17, 1972 - Five burglars are arrested inside the Watergate building in Washington while attempting to plant hidden microphones in the Democratic National Committee offices. Subsequent investigations will reveal they have ties to the Nixon White House.

June 28, 1972 - South Vietnamese troops begin a counter-offensive to retake Quang Tri Province, aided by U.S. Navy gunfire and B-52 bombardments.

June 30, 1972 - General Frederick C. Weyand replaces Gen. Abrams as MACV commander in Vietnam.

July 11, 1972 - NVA attack on An Loc is thwarted by South Vietnamese troops aided by B-52 air strikes.

July 13, 1972 - Paris peace talks resume.

July 14, 1972 - The Democrats choose Senator George McGovern of South Dakota as their presidential nominee. McGovern, an outspoken critic of the war, advocates "immediate and complete withdrawal."

July 18, 1972 - During a visit to Hanoi, actress Jane Fonda broadcasts anti-war messages via Hanoi Radio.

July 19, 1972 - South Vietnamese troops begin a major counter-offensive against NVA in Binh Dinh Province.

August 1, 1972 - Henry Kissinger meets again with Le Duc Tho in Paris

August 23, 1972 - The last U.S. combat troops depart Vietnam.

September 16, 1972 - Quang Tri City is recaptured by South Vietnamese troops.

September 29, 1972 - Heavy U.S. air raids against airfields in North Vietnam destroy 10 percent of their air force.

October 8, 1972 - The long-standing diplomatic stalemate between Henry Kissinger and Le Duc Tho finally ends as both sides agree to major concessions. The U.S. will allow North Vietnamese troops already in South Vietnam to remain there, while North Vietnam drops its demand for the removal of South Vietnam's President Thieu and the dissolution of his government.

Although Kissinger's staff members privately express concerns over allowing NVA troops to remain in the South, Kissinger rebuffs them, saying, "I want to end this war before the election."

October 22, 1972 - In Saigon, Kissinger visits President Thieu to discuss the peace proposal.

Meetings between Kissinger and Thieu go badly as an emotional Thieu adamantly opposes allowing North Vietnamese troops to remain indefinitely in South Vietnam. An angry Kissinger reports Thieu's reaction to President Nixon, who then threatens Thieu with a total cut-off of all American aid. But Thieu does not back down. Kissinger then returns to Washington.

October 22, 1972 - Operation Linebacker I ends. U.S. warplanes flew 40,000 sorties and dropped over 125,000 tons of bombs during the bombing campaign which effectively disrupted North Vietnam's Eastertide Offensive.

During the failed offensive, the North suffered an estimated 100,000 military casualties and lost half its tanks and artillery. Leader of the offensive, legendary General Vo Nguyen Giap, the victor at Dien Bien Phu, was then quietly ousted in favor of his deputy Gen. Van Tien Dung. 40,000 South Vietnamese soldiers died stopping the offensive, in the heaviest fighting of the entire war.

October 24, 1972 - President Thieu publicly denounces Kissinger's peace proposal.

October 26, 1972 - Radio Hanoi reveals terms of the peace proposal and accuses the U.S. of attempting to sabotage the settlement. At the White House, now a week before the presidential election, Henry Kissinger holds a press briefing and declares "We believe that peace is at hand. We believe that an agreement is in sight."

November 7, 1972 - Richard M. Nixon wins the presidential election in the biggest landslide to date in U.S. history.

November 14, 1972 - President Nixon sends a letter to President Thieu secretly pledging "to take swift and severe retaliatory action" if North Vietnam violates the proposed peace treaty.

November 30, 1972 - American troop withdrawal from Vietnam is completed, although there are still 16,000 Army advisors and administrators remaining to assist South Vietnam's military forces.

http://www.historyplace.com/unitedstates/vietnam/index-1969.html

APPENDIX 2

Phoenix Program Essay by Dale Kraken
"The Phoenix Program:
A Covert CIA Operation of the Vietnam War"

Phoenix Program Essay by Dale Kraken
"The Phoenix Program: A Covert CIA Operation of the Vietnam War"

Abstract

My thesis is that the classified Phoenix Program was a successful pacification program during the latter stages of the Vietnam War, and much of the Program's success could be attributed to the unconventional Provincial Reconnaissance Units (PRU) in the 44 provinces. Through primary and secondary sources, I proved the PRU were dedicated soldiers, with many strategies for gathering intelligence. They acquired a reputation as assassins, but most of their neutralizations were captures or Hoi Chanhs, and the kills they did make were on the battlefield. They were, man for man, the most effective fighting force in South Vietnam.

The Role of the Provincial Reconnaissance Units in the Phoenix Program of the Vietnam War

American forces reporting to the CIA included Navy Seals, Army Green Berets, and Army Military Intelligence. South Vietnamese forces reporting to the CIA included Regional Forces, Popular Forces, and the Provincial Reconnaissance Units (PRU). The Phoenix Program was a successful pacification program, and the PRU contributed a great deal to that success. The membership, structure, incentives, rules, and tactics by which the PRU operated were unconventional and unique in modern warfare.

The US made numerous bombing raids on North Vietnam, but they had no dramatic effect. It became apparent to the CIA that to defeat the communists, they would have to practice the same tactics that the Viet Cong used against them. That was the purpose of the Counter Terror Teams (CTT), the immediate forerunner of the PRU. In 1965, William Colby, then head of the Far East Division of the Clandestine Services, supervised the founding of the CIA's Counter Terror Teams. Vietnamese citizens filled the ranks, but the Counter Terror program was an American undertaking not affiliated with the South Vietnamese government. The CIA oversaw all aspects of the program, including recruiting, organizing, supplying, and paying the CTT (Marchietti and Marks, 245).

The Phoenix Program was born in 1967. It was the idea of William Colby, and he remains today as the person most closely associated with it. In most South Vietnamese villages, there was a legitimate village government, and then there was an illegitimate Viet Cong shadow government, peopled by civilian South Vietnamese communists, which in fact ruled the village. These illegitimate VCI-supported governments maintained their status with economic and physical threats, intimidating villagers to the point that they were afraid to turn any Viet Cong in to the South Vietnamese government. The VCI was the "rural apparatus on which the Viet Cong relied for recruits, food, money and asylum" (Karnow, 601).

Colby also oversaw the creation of Provincial Interrogation Centers (PIC). As the name suggests, a PIC was constructed in each of South Vietnam's 44 provinces. PICs were the site of interrogations, as well as much of the alleged torture that plagued the Phoenix Program's reputation (Karnow, 601). Actually, Viet Cong were generally uneducated and taken from families against their will. For many of the people brought in to the PICs, their first decent meal in a long time was enough to convince them to relinquish information and defect, says Nelson Brickham. Brickham was Chief of Field Operations for the CIA Special Branch, and he admitted to being one of the chief architects of the Phoenix Program (Personal Interview, 13 July 2000).

The CTT became the PRU in 1966. The PRU served the same purpose as their predecessors, except the name change gave the PRU a different image. The word "Terror" in "Counter Terror Teams" reflected badly on an already controversial program, so the CIA changed the name. The key word in the PRU name is reconnaissance, or information gathering. Both the CTT and the PRU received the reputation of "assassins" and "trained killers," but the fact is that they emphasized capture over kills because information gathering could only occur with a live person (Marchietti and Marks, 245).

"If a strict chain of command, a rank structure, and rigid rules make up military structure and discipline, then the PRU definitely was not part of the military ... an unconventional enemy called for unconventional tactics." That was precisely what the CIA was thinking when they created the PRU. They knew exactly for whom they were looking, and they generally did not have to venture far to locate them (Andrade, 172).

There were basically three types of South Vietnamese individuals that made up the PRU. The first type was those who had a fervent hatred of the communists on a personal level. A PRU adviser once said, "These were hard-bitten guys who were really ticked off by the communists. They had lost families and wanted revenge" (Andrade, 173). A large percentage of these anti-communists were actually former communists. The PRU were one of a few forces in the Government of Vietnam (GVN), if not the only one, that welcomed former communists into their ranks. "They needed a job, and when they came over all they knew how to do was fight. They didn't want to be farmers, so they tried to join the PRUs" (Moyar, 168).

Army of the Republic of [South] Vietnam (ARVN) deserters constituted the second type of soldier in the PRU. The CIA had adequate power to prevent the return of the deserters to Vietnamese control if the GVN attempted to order it (Moyar, 168).

ARVN deserters and anti-Communists accounted for the vast majority of PRU members; however, a third type, violent criminals, sometimes filtered into the ranks, preferring war service to prison. They were watched closely because of their potential to commit criminal acts, but it was undeniable that their effectiveness was paramount to the average PRU because they possessed great courage and were not afraid to die (Moyar, 168).

The PRU was not a large force, probably numbering somewhere in the vicinity of 4,000-6,000 members in all of South Vietnam. Each of the forty-four provinces supported one platoon, which was divided into three squads. Squad size varied greatly, from 30 to 60. Three factors dictated this small structure. First, very few were made of the "right stuff" for the PRUs. A PRU adviser noted that "it was very clannish. You really had to be a tough nut to get into the PRU and stay in." Secondly, the PRU worked in small groups because that was the key to military success. Third, strict security would ensure that Viet Cong spies would not make their way into the ranks of the PRU. In addition, creating too large a force would compromise the secrecy that, for the most part, hid PRU activities from disapproving Americans (Andrade, 173).

There were numerous incentives to join the PRU. PRU members received higher salaries than those working for the Government of Vietnam (GVN), and they received US medical treatment, a luxury for the South Vietnamese. They were rewarded for kills and captures and were sometimes even allowed to keep booty found during their mission. Residing in provincial capitals, they received good food and drink and were well protected from communist attacks. Despite the fact that PRU operations involved a great deal of danger, members suffered fewer deaths than other South Vietnamese units (Moyar, 168). Being in the PRU was essentially a privilege, explaining why the CIA could be quite selective in choosing members.

There was no official hierarchy within the PRU, but the advisors did have a chain of command. A PRU chief was the leader of a unit and directed the field operations, and his degree of aggressiveness usually determined the success of a unit. The PRU chief reported to the CIA province officer, who selected assignments. The province officers reported to the CIA regional officer, who reported to the CIA chief of station in Saigon, the head of the CIA in South Vietnam (Andrade, 176).

The mission of the PRU to gather intelligence and neutralize the VCI was accomplished through intense interrogation, which if unsuccessful could lead to torture until suspected Viet Cong confessed. There were many tactics in place to prevent torture. One of the intelligence gathering tactics employed in the Phoenix program was the Chieu Hoi (Open Arms) program, which offered amnesty to Viet Cong defectors. "Chieu Hoi personnel questioned the 'ralliers' about Viet Cong methods of operation, the identities of specific cadres, and other important topics. They indoctrinated the ralliers and then tried to get them to work for the GVN or resettle them in GVN areas" (Moyar, 36). Chieu Hoi was an integral part of Phoenix's intelligence gathering system.

When Chieu Hoi failed and suspected Viet Cong remained silent, the PRU relied on other means to make them talk. Since the PRU operated on good intelligence, they needed the Viet Cong alive in order to interrogate them; however, the PRU did not hesitate to kill their targets. Most Americans viewed this as assassination and murder, not caring to examine the situation any further. "The result of what PRUs did was not much different than body counts from search-and-destroy missions, aerial bombings, and artillery strikes. Both resulted in death to the enemy, but PRU operations were much more discerning than the massive affairs launched by conventional United States and ARVN forces" (Andrade, 175). The PRU sometimes killed surrendering communists and captured prisoners, but it usually occurred shortly after the battle, when emotions played a large role in their judgement (Moyar, 92).

An operation in Ben Cat district of Binh Duong Province (just north of Saigon) characterized a typical PRU mission. The initial intelligence originated with a Hoi Chanh, who defected through the Chieu Hoi program. The PRU discovered that the assistant party secretary to the Chau Thanh Viet Cong district committee was in a tunnel. PRU personnel moved in and interrogated him on the spot, and he released the whereabouts of another tunnel holding a former assistant party secretary and the Viet Cong security section chief. The PRU advanced on that location, and after a short exchange of gunfire, these Viet Cong officials surrendered just like their comrade. The PRU captured documents and brought them to the PIC, and the cycle of intelligence gathering and suspect apprehension would continue (Andrade, 188). Sometimes, however, the suspects did not surrender so easily, and the PRU resorted to brutal methods.

A major factor in the Phoenix controversy was the alleged torture inflicted by the PRU, although most American sources deny that it ever happened. Jerome Waldie, a congressman, visited Vietnam to uncover secret torture practices and provide further justification for the United States to disengage itself from the Vietnam War, yet he reported no sign of abuse. Michael Walsh was a PRU adviser who sat in on interrogations at the PICs, and he emphasized that they "were experts in their field, and they used their minds to conquer the spirit of those they were questioning" (Moyar, 90). Warren Milberg, who served in Vietnam from July 1967 until April 1969 as Province Officer in Charge in Quang Tri Province, overseeing the PRU and Rural Development Cadre team operations, stated that no torture occurred as a matter of policy, and he was personally unaware of any abuses by the Quang Tri PRU (Correspondence, 2 August 2000).

Though Americans generally said that torture occurred very seldom if at all, many Vietnamese would strongly contest that. An anonymous Vietnamese employee at the National Police Convalescence Center offered an impression of the situation. "I saw prisoners hit with sticks while hung by their feet; others had nails pulled out and soapy water forced down their mouths until they choked. Sometimes they used the electric crank with wires attached to the ears, nose, or genitals. Even with the women. They attached the wires to their breasts." In another incident, a former secret policeman at a PIC admitted to participating in torture and confirmed that a woman had a hard rubber club shoved into her vagina (Drosnin, 21).

As stated in the account above, torture was used to get information from stubborn people; however, innocent people were rounded up as well, which some suggest were intended to fulfill a neutralization quota imposed by the CIA. One source claimed two lieutenants became conscientious objectors after learning they would have to neutralize fifty VCI per month. Warren Milberg said "various kinds of quotas were often received from Da Nang, who probably received them from Saigon, who received them from Washington. We mostly attempted to do our jobs as best as we could under very difficult circumstances. As a result, not much attention was paid to quotas" (Correspondence, 2 August 2000).

The cells that the suspected Viet Cong were placed in were often called "tiger cages," and the most infamous prison was Con Son, where these 5x9 foot pits with grated ceilings were found. The prisoners requested water, but instead were showered with lime, which burned their skin and blinded at least one woman. In PICs, the maximum "legal" amount of time the prisoners could be held was 45 days, but they were usually held until they paid their bribe or confessed. The term "confessed" is used loosely, because those tortured were often innocent people who had no real information to give. A former Vietnamese officer revealed a disturbing saying of his department: "If they are innocent, beat them until they are guilty" (Drosnin, 22).

Derrill Ballenger served two terms in Vietnam and had three assignments. From July 1967 to July 1968 he was G2 (intelligence) advisor to the 22nd Army of Vietnam Infantry Division; from September 1970 to January 1971 he was Special Assistant to the Commanding General, Combat Security, Quinhon Province; and from January 1971 to September 1971, Commander, Intelligence Collection Detachment, 3rd Military Intelligence Battalion, 525th Military Intelligence Group (United States Army in Vietnam). These assignments provided him knowledge of the Phoenix Program. Ballenger had personal knowledge of terrorist torture and assassination of friendly/hamlet district people by the Viet Cong, so he did not doubt that the torture was returned "in kind," but he had no specific knowledge of innocents being killed (Correspondence, August 2000). Warren Milberg said that innocents were killed, but that they were accidental deaths and not ones that occurred as a matter of planning or policy (Correspondence, 2 August 2000).

It is widely accepted—even by William Colby himself—that Phoenix was not a complete success. However, many of those people who accept that assessment are just as ready to admit that it was an effective aspect of the US effort against the VCI. Colby mentioned that Phoenix was a public program, not a secret assassination operation, and to support this, he cites the fact that the Vietnamese Prime Minister launched the program publicly and explained its goals to the people. Phoenix supported peaceful resolution, putting up "wanted" posters. The posters did not say "Wanted: Dead or Alive" like in the 19th century American West; rather, they named VCI that Phoenix wanted to have surrender through Chieu Hoi. Phoenix made its intentions clear when it wanted to perform a mission, notifying the Village Chiefs of operations in their area so they could provide information about the area to help the PRU do the best job possible (*Honorable Men*, 273).

Derrill Ballenger opined on the successes and failures of the Phoenix Program. He believed Phoenix succeeded because it "created fear and apprehension within the VCI, removed important leaders and terrorists from the VCI, and it provided friendly forces with a sense of 'deserved justice'." He stated the Phoenix Program also had its weaknesses: Its "actions were sometimes based more on suspicion than hard intelligence, resulting in the deaths of innocent people; it was sometimes used to remove political opponents who were not actual VC personnel; and it was 'stooping' to the level of the enemy" (Correspondence, August 2000).

Considering the massive scope of the Phoenix Program, it is obvious that innocent people were killed. On the battlefield, those people were simply in the wrong place at the wrong time. In terms of torture, saying that none occurred would almost certainly be erroneous, but it was never an approved method of interrogation. Any torture that did occur was inflicted by individuals or groups acting on their own. Even considering the fact that torture happened, the Phoenix Program did accomplish the things it was meant to do. The VCI later described to the CIA the success of Phoenix in neutralizing a large number of VCI. North Vietnamese General Tran Do called it "extremely destructive," and Foreign Minister Nguyen Co Thach said Phoenix "wiped out many of our bases." A great host of others supported these claims, admitting that thousands of true VCI were neutralized as a result of Phoenix (Karnow, 602).

To give a completely accurate response to the question of whether the Phoenix Program was a success or a failure, there would have to be 44 answers, since Phoenix success varied from province to province. Both Warren Milberg and Nelson Brickham agree that the success or failure of the Phoenix Program in each province was due in large part to the province chief. In Quang Tri Province, according to Milberg, the Vietnamese province chief, a colonel in the ARVN, had much control over the Phoenix activities in his province. After all, this was a joint US/Vietnamese program. In some provinces, the Province Chief was moral and used the forces to fight the Viet Cong, while in other provinces, like Quang Tri, the chief was corrupt and would use the PRU and other assets for his own political purposes, whatever those may have been (Brickham, Personal Interview, 13 July 2000) (Milberg, Correspondence, 23 July 2000).

Overall, however, the Phoenix program was a success. Milberg said, as did William Colby, that the program to neutralize the VCI was successful because it forced the North Vietnamese to abandon their basic attempt at insurgency in South Vietnam and to adopt a more traditional limited war strategy. The effectiveness of the Phoenix Program is apparent after studying the statistics. Colby stated that about 20,587 VCI had been killed, 29,978 were captured, and 17,717 had taken advantage of Chieu Hoi. Out of those numbers, 7,408 Viet Cong were captured and 4,407 were killed by the PRU; only 179 PRU members died. Those are excellent statistics for a force that numbered only several thousand men (Andrade 184). That totals 68,282 VCI neutralized, of which about 70% were not killed. Most of those that *were* killed were killed in the heat of combat, and 88% of those were killed by conventional, non-PRU forces (*Lost Victory*, 331). Therefore, the PRU reputation for assassination seems to be undeserved. A "midnight assassination"—the term given to sneaking into a hut at night and killing people in their sleep—plagued the PRUs' reputation, but if it happened at all, it was an extremely rare occurrence.

When compared with other unit types within the Phoenix Program, PRU effectiveness was even more evident. Statistics from 1968 in the province of Long An indicate that the ARVN had a 66% desertion rate, while the Regional Force, a district level military unit, had a 29% desertion rate. The Popular Force, a village level military unit, had an 18% desertion rate, and in the PRU desertion was 0%. In a ratio of enemies killed in action to friendly killed in action, the ARVN had 2.5 (2.5 times more kills than deaths among themselves), the Regional Force had 3.2, the Popular Force had 3.1, and the PRU had 6.6. These statistics indicate that the PRU were dedicated soldiers who worked hard to do their job well and were extremely effective (Race, 231).

The PRU were composed of Vietnamese, but their advisers were American. As Derrill Ballenger states, some advisers were "contract cowboys" who "ignored good intelligence" and "wanted to play Rambo," but most carried out their duties effectively (Correspondence, August 2000). As the years progressed, it became readily apparent that the leadership of the US advisers was an important factor in determining the PRU success. In the final years of the war, around 1973, the PRU were placed within the structure of the National Police, who were under the supervision of the GVN, and this effectively reduced both the level of US advisory and financial support. This was done as part of a "Vietnamization" program, which aimed to make the South Vietnamese more self-reliant by letting them control their own operations. "They became part of the GVN's unwieldy and often corrupt and incompetent system" and "degenerated into bands of armed thugs who extorted money from the local population at will" (Andrade, 185). Now that the most effective fighting force in the Phoenix Program had been reduced to a horde of renegade criminals, the Phoenix had lost its wings, and it was only a matter of time before it would come crashing to the ground.

The PRU were the most effective force countering the VCI during the entire Vietnam War and specifically within the Phoenix Program. "No one could have disputed the Phoenix Program's effectiveness if everyone had performed as well as the PRU." Their operational professionalism and effective use of intelligence made them the best Phoenix force by far, boasting 422 VCI neutralizations for every 1,000 PRU. The National Police, the next best organization in man-to-man neutralizations, neutralized only 36 VCI for every 1,000 men. Unfortunately, because of their small numbers, the PRU only accounted for about 7% of all VCI neutralizations (Andrade, 187). If the number of PRU had been larger, however, they would have possibly been less effective, both because of greater chance of VCI infiltration into PRU ranks and a greater chance of disorganization. Rumors of torture and killing of innocents dogged the PRU and Phoenix's reputation, and chances are that isolated incidents did occur, but it was war, and sometimes a combatant doesn't have time to think before shooting someone, or emotions may overtake his judgement. The American public didn't consider the fact that if it were their town being taken over by hostile forces, they would be fighting in the exact same manner. The Vietnam War was an unconventional war, and the methods used by the PRU were similarly unconventional. A vast array of organizations affirmed PRU effectiveness, ranging from the CIA to the North Vietnamese and Viet Cong, who saw the forces of Phoenix decimate the ranks of their shadow governments. The PRU fought with skill and precision, but they were dependent on the US for leadership and financial resources, important factors in determining PRU success. Discontinuance of US support ultimately led to the end of the previously unstoppable PRU fighting force and the demise of the Phoenix Program. Ashes to ashes, dust to dust.

Sources

Andrade, Dale. *Ashes to Ashes: The Phoenix Program and the Vietnam War*. Lexington, Massachusetts: Lexington Books, 1990.

Ballenger, Derrill. Correspondence. August 2000.

Brickham, Nelson. Personal Interview: 13 July 2000.

Colby, William, and Peter Forbath. *Honorable Men: My Life in the CIA*. New York: Simon and Schuster, 1978.

Colby, William, with James McCargar. *Lost Victory: A Firsthand Account of America's Sixteen-year Involvement in Vietnam*. Chicago: Contemporary Books, 1989.

Drosnin, Michael. "Phoenix: The CIA's Biggest Assassination Program." *New Times*, August 1975, 16-24.

Karnow, Stanley. *Vietnam: A History*. New York: Viking, 1983.

Marchetti, Victor, and John D. Marks. *The CIA and the Cult of Intelligence*. New York: Alfred A. Knopf, 1974.

McGehee, Ralph. *Deadly Deceits: My 25 years in the CIA*. New York: Sheridan Square Publications, 1983.

Milberg, Warren. Correspondences. 23 July 2000 and 2 August 2000.

Moyar, Mark. *Phoenix and the Birds of Prey*. Annapolis: Naval Institute Press, 1997.

Race, Jeffrey. *War Comes to Long An*. Berkeley, California: University of California Press, 1972

http://www.writing.com/main/view_item/item_id/583086-The-Phoenix-Program

APPENDIX 3

Training Materials
Military Assistance Security Advisor Course

JFK Center for Unconventional Warfare
1972

SUMMARY SHEET

To enable the student to explain the principles that determine insurgent capabilities in the internal defense situation.

a. <u>Capabilities are</u> defined as <u>courses of action aimed at the destruction</u> of the government <u>through influence</u> upon the people, the government, the insurgents themselves, and the relationships between them.

b. In determining enemy capabilities five questions need to be answered: <u>What, Where, When, How,</u> and Which. By applying these questions to the current situation and producing pertinent, valid, and complete answers to them, a truthful and complete estimate of the insurgent's capabilities and intentions will be achieved.

c. Insurgent capabilities can be classified into three areas:

(1) <u>Basic capabilities</u> are those insurgent courses of action aimed directly and immediately toward the destruction of the government. The basic courses of action are <u>nonviolent,</u> terrorist, guerrilla operations, and <u>standard tactical operations.</u>

(a) <u>Nonviolent</u> action will be directed toward bringing about changes in the political, economic, and social framework of the society--frequently <u>through psychological means.</u>

(b) <u>Terroristic</u> activities are particularly <u>useful for gaining control</u> over the populace.

(c) The insurgents normally will use terror as one of their main weapons during any phase of the insurgency, but insurgents <u>do not engage in guerrilla operations until they have developed a military capability</u> of at least squad or platoon size.

(2) Supporting capabilities pertain directly to the insurgent themselves and only indirectly to the downfall of the government. The <u>support capabilities can be categorized into four general areas:</u> intelligence and security, recruitment and retention organization and training, and finance and logistics.

(a) <u>Intelligence and security are absolutely essential for the insurgent's survival.</u> The insurgent must gain intelligence of his enemy and secure himself from capture and neutralization.

(b) The insurgent must also possess a capability of recruiting personnel for his organization and retaining them. The types of people recruited into the insurgent's movement and how they are recruited depend largely upon the movement's stage of development.

(c) The insurgent's leaders must possess the ability to create an effective organizational structure and maintain a continuous political indoctrination and leadership training programs.

(d) Through finance and logistical activities, the insurgent must develop a capability to supply and move his forces.

(3) Reinforcing capabilities are those insurgent capabilities which enable the insurgent to reinforce any type of activity and thus significantly change the conflict being developed.

d. A successful application of these concepts rests with the ability to analyze the enemy. The manner in which to do this can be outlined by others, but the final product, valid intelligence regarding a particular insurgent's capabilities, rests with you.

VCI ORGANIZATION AND MODUS OPERANDI

1280
Oct 71

SUMMARY SHEET

The objective of this lesson was to enable the Military Assistance Security Advisor Course student to provide advice and technical assistance to a Vietnamese counterpart pertaining to the identification and neutralization of members of the Viet Cong Infrastructure organization.

a.   The three elements of the Viet Cong insurgency are the military--the Liberation Army, the party--the People's Revolutionary Party, and the front-- the National Front for the Liberation of South Vietnam (NFLSUV).

b.   A front is a specific purpose organization, innocuous in appearance, including Communist Party participation, and eventually coming under disguised party control. At the local level, the front consists of mass associations, the most important of which are the Farmer's Association, the Women's Association, and the Youth Association. Fronts are used to justify and legitimize causes, to neutralize opposition elements, to mobilize and manipulate the masses, and to disguise party control.

c.   The People's Revolutionary Party (PRP)--the Communist Party of South Vietnam--is the primary agency that controls the VC insurgency. The PRP, however, is only a regional extension of the North Vietnamese Communist Labor (Lao Dong) Party. The PRP receives its direction and control from Hanoi through PRP headquarters--the Central Office for South Vietnam (COSVN).

d.   The VC organizational structure is that of a parallel hierarchy in which each echelon consists of military units, a bureaucratic party structure, and the front. The PRP strictly controls this structure through the concepts of interlocking directorates and reverse representation (democratic centralism). Interlocking directorates is the placement of dedicated party members into key leadership positions of the parallel hierarchies and interlocking the positions of leadership in such a way as to insure party control. In general, a party member will hold leadership positions concurrently in at least two of the three elements of the organization at any particular echelon. Reverse representation is the practice of characterizing the leader of any party body as a delegate from a superior body, imposed upon a subordinated lesser body, to assure higher authorities that their policy is being carried out.

e.   Along with the front, the VC have attempted to form peoples's liberation committees, "elected" bodies controlled by the party, which would parallel the GVN at every echelon. At national level, the PRP has formed the Provisional Revolutionary Government, which pretends to be the duly constituted government of South Vietnam and under which the people's liberation committees will be located.

f.   The objective of the PRP is to gain control of a willing South Vietnamese people. To achieve this end, the PRP established a functional, bureaucratic organization--the Viet Cong Infrastructure (VCI). The VCI is that

SS-1

145

political and administrative apparatus through which the Viet Cong control or seek to control the South Vietnamese people. The VCI attempt to gain control of the people to such an extent that certain desired responses from the populace are assured. These desired responses suggest four submissions of the VCI: intelligence, supplies, recruits, and labor.

g.   A VCI can be defined as a trained, civilian, political cadre. Criteria for classification as a member of the VCI are function-leadership or policymaking training--the preparation an individual has received which qualifies him for a specific function whether filling that position or not; and party membership-- full or probationary membership in the PRP qualifies an individual for classi- fication as a VCI. Thus the VCI includes all PRP members, chiefs, and members of the party's functional elements, leadership of the executive committees of the parallel front organizations, and political officers of VC military units. VCI have been divided by MACV into two categories: A and B. In general, a category A VCI must be a member of the PRP or a leader of one of the party's functional sections. Category B VCI are the members of these sections. This categorization is used for judicial processing purposes.

h.   The Cadre Affairs Section is a group of two or three hard-core VCI cadre responsible for the initial development of the VCI organization within a village. Usually they are sent from outside the village. Upon arrival in the village, they will operate covertly. At the final stage, when the VCI have gained control, this may change. Just as with any underground, the initial ac- tivities of this section must be guided by the utmost security precautions.

i.   Initially, if they do not exist already, the Cadre Affairs Section (CAS) will begin to form the populace into several associations whose basis will be the people's needs and/or grievances. After the associations have been formed, the CAS, over a period of time (months or even years), will scrutinize the members of the associations to single out a selected few potential leaders who are sympathetic to the VC cause. To further test their loyalties, the CAS will force these individuals to commit themselves by the performance of illegal acts. They will then be drawn into the infrastructure. After this infrastruc- ture has five members, it is no longer called a CAS but is called a party chap- ter.

j.   As the infrastructure grows, it will place its members in key positions of leadership within the associations. At the same time, the party chapter will begin to form the framework of the VCI machinery, dividing itself into leader- ship elements for security, finance and economy, proselyting, and military af- fairs. The initial CAS members (3) will retain ultimate control. Once the above have been accomplished, the VCI will covertly begin to manipulate the associations towards the VC's needs. At this time, taxes will start to be col- lected and the beginnings of a local guerrilla unit will appear. Through pro- paganda schemes, and the manipulation of the masses by the VCI leaders, the VCI will finally gain control of the populace. It is the party's objective to gain control of a willing populace. If this cannot be done, however, the VCI will

SS-2

146

revert to force to gain control. At this time, the VCI structure has matured into a viable organization.

k. The following factors have promoted the existence of the VCI and their influence over the people:

(1) As compared to the continuous changeover of GVN bureaucrats in the last decade, the VCI organization has been quite stable, allowing it to increase the sophistication of its organization and to advance its operational techniques.

(2) The cellular structure of the VCI organization provides a controlled and limited knowledge of the organization by its members.

(3) The VCI organization is highly flexible and can be adapted to meet the needs of any particular situation.

(4) The VCI exploit popular grievances to gain the support of a willing populace.

(5) Terrorism by the VCI inhibits the population from disclosing the VCI and from actively joining the GVN.

(6) The VCI's extensive intelligence and counterintelligence apparatus allows for its operational success and makes it very difficult for the GVN to identify and neutralize the VCI.

l. The VCI, as other Communist organizations, is ruled by committees; Communist doctrine does not allow all authority to be vested in a single individual. The committees then are the policymaking elements. Underneath the committees there are functional elements or sections that have been organized to perform specific tasks to further the party committee's organizations.

APPENDIX 4

Delta MR-4 Phoenix/Phung Hoang Program

Office of the Deputy for CORDS

MACDR-CR-PX   16 May 1972

SUBJECT: Phung Hoang Reorganization

SEE DISTRIBUTION

1. Attached are translations of the Presidential Decree and implementing directives recently promulgated at national level regarding the organization and functions of the Phung Hoang effort.

2. The attached documents do not address several important questions which will require resolution prior to National Police assumption of responsibility for the Phung Hoang Program. Further implementing instructions are expected from National Police Command and will be forwarded as soon as they become available.

FOR THE DEPCORDS:

3 Incl

1. Presidential Decree
   210/TT/SL, 12 Apr 72
2. Prime Ministerial Order
   398/ND/Th.T/VP, 18 Apr 72
3. Prime Ministerial Dir.
   050.MT/Th.T/VP, 18 Apr 72

ROBERT G. CRAMER
COL, GS
PHUNG HOANG Advisor, DRAC

DISTRIBUTION:
C
Plus
1 - ea PSA
5 - PSD
15- Phung Hoang

APPENDIX 5

Delta MR-4 Phoenix Neutralization Briefing Notes and G2 Incident Reports

PHUNG HOANG DIVISION
DMAC, IV MR

Operations Office

1 June 1972

TO: COL CRAMER

Total Operations: 128
Total A&B Neutralized: 25 (9 "A", 16 "B")
   District: 3
   Village: 16
   Hamlet: 6

G-2 Briefing: 10 Incidents

A hamlet was infiltrated in Kien Phong but no results were recorded, a GMC truck was destroyed when it hit a mine as part of a convoy moving to Kien Luong from Rach Gia in Kien Giang Province, and 13 PF moved from their OB to another one when it received a "G.A." in Ba Xuyen.

Post Briefing Notes:

Artillery that has been damaged still needs to used and much of it can be repaired. G-4 is to make sure they get the needed repairs. G-4 is to coordinate with operations at Moc Hoa.

CPT ██, MI
Ass't Operations Officer

PHUNG HOANG DIVISION
DMAC, IV MR

Operations Office

2 June 1972

TO: COL CRAMER

Total Operations: 148
Total A&B Neutralized: 22
   Province level: 3
   District level: 2
   Village level: 14
   Hamlet level: 3

G-2 Briefing: 13 Incidents

1. KP: A grenade was thrown at the HQ of the "Th Phong" Campaign, 2 km S of Cao Lanh. 1 PF was wounded and 1 PSDF was killed.
2. VL: 1 PF and 7 PSDF of My Hoa Village, 8 km SE of Binh Mirh gave their weapons to the VC and all of them are missing.

Post Briefing Notes:

1. Seven damaged artillery tubes were reported. Repair is being conducted through Ordnance.
2. In response to a question as to why a SGM was commanding LFs at Hai Yen, it was stated that a Police CPT had just been sent there. Then it was stated that policemen at hamlet and village levels should be wearing uniforms rather than civilian clothing. An MSS member was to be replaced in Cau Ngang District, Vinh Binh.
3. G-3 is to meet GEN Nghi at Chi Leng at 1000 with two other named COLs.

CPT ██, MI
Ass't Operations Officer

3 June 1972

TO: COL CRAMER [signature]

Total Operations: 148
Total A&B Neutralized: 16, all at village level.

G-2 Briefing: 19 incidents in MR4
1. KP: Hamlet 16 km NE Hong Ngu was attacked. NEG.
2. PD: Binh Tuy Air Base was hit with 3 rds 107.
   Ammo dump was hit, NEG casualties.
3. BL: Hamlet attacked 17 km SE Gia Rai. 2 FSDF KIA,
   18 FSDF WIA, 4 FSDF MIA.
4. AX: Betrayer in FF OB, 11 km N Dam Doi (UNK)

F6 Campaign: 29 picked up yesterday—Chau Doc had 15.

Post Briefing Notes:
1. Status of artillery was given.
2. COL Son was ordered to begin the Binh Tay campaign again by 5 June.
3. Logistics problem at Hong Ngu was discussed. It was stated that gasoline is there already. GEN NGHI said he wanted a 5 day supply of ammunition at Moc Hoa. Sufficient gasoline must be at Hong Ngu for tracked vehicles.

[signature]
DAVID L. LUCKETT
MAJ, MI
Operations Officer

---

4 June 1972

TO: COL CRAMER [signature]

Total Operations: 137
Total A&B Neutralized: 22 (5 "A", 17 "B")
  Province: 1
  District: 1
  Village: 19
  Hamlet: 1

F6 Results: 32 Captured for 3 JUN; 61 Total since 1 JUN.
3,324 grand total.

G-2 Briefing: 19 Incidents.
1. KG: Bridge (WS136004) on TL 12 received 50% damage from a mine. 1 PF KIA.
2. PD: Binh Tuy ammo dump was detonated by an unk wpn. 1 ARVN KIA, investigation underway.
3. EX: G.A./traitor at FF OP, 6 km N Ke Sach. 3PF left the OP and rest of results unreported.
4. AX: G.A., FF OP, 3 km W Ca Mau. 4 KIA, 2 WIA, 2 MIA.
5. CD: Hamlet 5 km SE Tinh Bien hit with 15 rds M79 FSDF position in hamlet, 13 km SW Tinh Bien received small arms fire. Both incidents had NEG results.

Post Briefing Notes:
1. Howitzer damage status: 5 tubes 105 and 3 tubes 155. GEN Nghi said howitzer tubes must be repaired within 48 hours. They have the parts and the technicians; all that is lacking is coordination of transportation.
2. On Monday G-1 is to report on total manpower resources for May that were drafted, etc.
3. POLWAR is to initiate a campaign to commemorate [blacked out] which is 19 June. Armed Forces Day The campaign is [blacked out] Operations Officer aimed at ARVN, RF, PF units and sectors are to receive

PHUNG HOANG DIVISION
DMAC, IV MR

Operations Office

5 June 1972

TO: COL CRAMER [signature]

Total Operations: 146
Total A&B Neutralized: 14 (2 "A", 12 "B")
District level: 2
Village level: 12

F6 Results: 57 Capt. on 4 June; overall total is 118 for the new phase and grand total is 3,381.

G-2 Briefing: 6 incidents.
Sa Dec had a bad overrun of a FF OB in which 4 traitors combined with a ground attack to kill 14 other FF and cause 40% OB damage, 5 km SE Duc Ton.

Manpower, PF/RF Conversion and Howitzer damage briefings were given. GEN Nghi wants sectors to report directly to him if they cannot fulfill PF/RF conversion requirements.

GEN Nghi stated that he wanted POLWAR to insure that propaganda leaflets were dropped in the proper locations and that the troops were instructed in leaflet distribution so that the enemy will get hold of them.

COL Son was asked to attempt to raise police results on the weekends. Coordination should exist between sectors and police. Police should go on Dong Khoi operations. Operations need to be conducted into the less secure areas, while maintaing operations in urban areas.

[signature]
CPT ██, MI
ASSISTANT Operations Officer

PHUNG HOANG DIVISION
DMAC, IV MR

Operations Office

6 June 1972

TO: COL CRAMER [signature]

Total Operations: 134
Total A & B Neutralized: 17
District: 3
Village: 14

F6 Results: 24 Captured from 5 June; 142 Captured since 1 June; Grand Total 3,405.

G-2: 13 Incidents
The only significant incident was in An Xuyen in which commo was lost to a FF OB. Two platoons of FF reported that all 23 men in the OB were missing.

[signature]
CPT ██, MI
ASSISTANT Operations Officer

PHUNG HOANG DIVISION
DMAC, IV MR

Operations Office

7 June 1972

TO: COL CRAMER RJC

Total Operations: 163
Total A&B Neutralized: 25 (7 "A", 18 "B")
Region: 1
District: 2
Village: 18
Hamlet: 4

F-6 Results: 52 for 6 June; 194 for June; 3,457 Total.

G-2 Briefing: 15 incidents all of minor significance.

Post Briefing Notes:
1. The escape of 17 soldiers from the VC in Chuong Thien is commendable and GEN Nghi wants them to have some time off to help raise their morale. Procedural policy was discussed in which GEN Nghi prescribed that PSYOPS, Province S-2, MSS and G-2 all become involved in acquiring information, raising morale and making sure they are not kept in custody for a long time.
2. G-1 is to establish a chart of results of RF & PF conscription and recruiting.
3. An IG investigation is to be conducted into the affairs of the Commanding Officer of the 7th ENG GP.
4. COL Son was instructed to conduct a campaign to raise morale in the ranks, to set discipline and apply orders regarding HL, F6 and Binh Tay. Prizes are to be set up to honor the best policeman in MR4. Additional prizes, rewards or medals are to be established for those who obtain results on operations. MSS is to have closer cooperation with friendly troops. If there are two incidents a month in w/which a Penetration agent was involved, the Commander of MSS will be personally responsible and will be replaced. If agents ██████ Operations Officer ████, MI put in custody and/or ███ will be

discovered, give suitable rewards. Replacement of poor

PHUNG HOANG DIVISION
DMAC, IV MR

Operations Office

8 June 1972

TO: COL CRAMER RJC

Total Operations: 146
Total A&B Neutralized: 21 (5 "A", 16 "B")
District: 2
Village: 13
Hamlet: 6

F-6 Results: 72 for 7 June; 266 since 1 June; 3,529 Total. Kien Hoa and An Giang - O.

G-2 Briefing: 18 Incidents
Attacks on hamlets occurred in Ba Xuyen and Chau Doc, and the VC infiltrated a wedding party in VL and killed one civilian.

Post Briefing Notes:
1. GEN Nghi now wants a Binh Tay briefing and a Phung Hoang briefing every two weeks by sectors and subsectors.
2. G-2 and G-3 are to coordinate on Dong Khoi operations and send memos to sectors with low results when the operations should have achieved something.

CPT ██, MI
Assistant Operations Officer

PHUNG HOANG DIVISION
DMAC, IV MR

Operations Office

8 June 1972

TO: COL CRAMER [signature]

Total Operations: 146
Total A&B Neutralized: 21 (5 "A", 16 "B")
  District: 2
  Village: 13
  Hamlet: 6

F-6 Results: 72 for 7 June; 266 since 1 June; 3,529 Total. Kien Hoa ▬ and An Giang - 0.

G-2 Briefing: 18 Incidents
Attacks on hamlets occurred in Ba Xuyen and Chau Doc, and the VC infiltrated a wedding party in VL and killed one civilian.

Post Briefing Notes:
1. GEN Nghi now wants a Binh Tuy briefing and a Phung Hoang briefing every two weeks by sectors and subsectors.
2. G-2 and G-3 are to coordinate on Dong Khoi operations and send memos to sectors with low results when the operations should have achieved something.

[signature] CPT ▬, MI
ASSISTANT Operations Officer

PHUNG HOANG DIVISION
DMAC, IV MR

Operations Office

7 June 1972

TO: COL CRAMER [signature]

Total Operations: 163
Total A&B Neutralized: 25 (7 "A", 18 "B")
  Region: 1
  District: 2
  Village: 18
  Hamlet: 4

F-6 Results: 52 for 6 June; 194 for June; 3,457 Total.

G-2 Briefing: 15 incidents all of minor significance.

Post Briefing Notes:
1. The escape of 17 soldiers from the VC in Chuong Thien is commendable and GEN Nghi wants them to have some time off to help raise their morale. Procedural policy was discussed in which GEN Nghi prescribed that PSYOPS, Province S-2, MSS and G-2 all become involved in acquiring information, raising morale and making sure they are not kept in custody for a long time.
2. G-1 is to establish a chart of results of RF & PF conscription and recruiting.
3. An IG investigation is to be conducted into the affairs of the Commanding Officer of the 7th ENG GP.
4. COL Son was instructed to conduct a campaign to raise morale in the ranks, to set discipline and apply orders regarding FM, F6 and Binh Tuy. Prizes are to be set up to honor the best policeman in MR4. Additional prizes, rewards or medals are to be established for those who obtain results on operations. MSS is to have closer cooperation with friendly troops. If there are two incidents a month in which a penetration agent was involved, the Commander of ▬ MSS will be personally responsible and ▬ will be ▬ Put in custody and/or ▬. If agents are ▬ replaced. [signature] ASSISTANT Operations Officer ▬, MI ▬ get. discovered, give suitable rewards. Replacement of poor

PHUNG HOANG DIVISION
DMAC, IV MR

Operations Office

9 June 1972

TO: COL CRAMER [signature]

Total Operations: 156
Total A&B Inactivated: 30 (7 "A", 23 "B")
  Province: 1
  District: 3
  Village: 25
  Hamlet: 1

F-6 Results: 53 (8 June); 319 since 1 JUN; 3,580 Total.

G-2 Briefing: 24 Incidents.
DT: Convoy hit mines 12 km and 15 km NW Gai Be. 1 truck received 80% damage. No casualties.
VL: 2 separate OPs received G.A., and a hamlet revd 12 rds 61 mm. 3 PF were killed in the attack on an OP 10 km E Tra Om; the other G.A. had UNK results.
VB: PF OP 4 km SE Cang Long revd G.A. 1 VC Killed, NEG F
KG: An Phuoc village infiltrated, 9 km S Kien Thanh, 5 PSDF Killed, 3 PSDF Wounded.
CT: Long Binh Hamlet infiltrated, 7 NE Long My—lost 1 carbine.

No Post Briefing Notes.

PHUNG HOANG DIVISION
DMAC, IV MR

Operations Office

10 June 1972

TO: COL CRAMER [signature]

Total Operations: 156
Total A&B Neutralized: 25 (7 "A", 18 "B")
  District: 3
  Village: 18
  Hamlet: 4

F-6 Results: 46 (9 JUN); 365 since 1 JUN; 3,679 Total.

G-2 Briefing: 25 incidents
6 Subsectors and 2 Province towns were mortared/G.A.
Subsectors mortared: Tuyen Nhon (KT); Cai Be (DT); Kien Binh (KG); and Phuoc Long (BL). The attack on Phuoc Long resulted in 3 ARVN WIA and 5 VC KIA.
Subsectors mortared with G.A.: Thoi Binh (AX) - UNK results; Tuyen Binh (KT) - UNK.
Province Towns mortared: Moc Hoa (KB) - UNK; Bac Lieu (BL) - NEG.
CD: A village was hit with small arms fire, 16 km N An Phu and a hamlet was infiltrated, 9 km SE Tinh Binh.
KG: G.A. PF OP, 4 km S Kien Binh. 1 VC Killed, 2 PF-K
BL: RF OP, mortar/G.A., 10 km NW BL. 1 RF Killed.
BL: G.A., PF OP, 6 km SW Gia Rai. Killed were 1 PF, 1 National Police, 1 PSDF.

Post Briefing Notes:
1. G-1 is to issue message to sectors that beginning in July, all troops attached to subsectors from sectors will cease. Do not attach RF to other branches. Also make plans for Division not to have detachments sent up, but may detach elements to lower levels.
2. Binh Tay results are poor and GEN Nghi stated that better results must be obtained. Also the rewards and promotion program must be immediately implemented. From now on all [redacted] problems will be [redacted] solved in one week.

[signature]
████, MI
Assistant Operations Officer

APPENDIX 6

Delta MR-4 G2 Intelligence Summary Enemy Activity
(April to December 1972)

VIETNAM ENEMY ACTIVITY REPORT

APRIL TO NOVEMBER 1972

Military Assistance Command Director for Intelligence

South Vietnamese Military Region 4 (Delta)

(Declassified, Pages A55-60)

http://www.vietnam.ttu.edu/star/images/107/1070703001e.pdf

April 1 to June 30, 1972

During the first half of April the most significant enemy activity took place in the tri-border area of Kien Tuong, Dinh Tuong, and Kien Phong Provinces (VC Military Region 2). There the 88th NVA Regiment was involved in an effort to wrest from friendly control the area generally north of Base Area 470. By month's end he had succeeded in this [effort.] [O]perations during month in both the triborder area and western Chuong Thien Province were apparently preparatory in nature, with the objectives of consolidating base areas and securing lines of communication prior to large unit actions. Along the Kien Tuong/Kien Phong Province border in particular, activity indicated the possibility of additional enemy troop infiltration.

May enemy activity in the Delta was at a lower level than in April, but continued to be elevated in comparison with prior months. Activity was greatest in three areas: the triborder area, northwestern Kien Giang Province, "and western Chuong Thien Province. In the first area it appeared that two enemy regiments were coordinating their efforts to attack district towns. Route

163

4, and other lines of communication. Prisoners and captured documents indicated increased enemy infiltration into the area. In northwest Kien Giang Province a prisoner and captured documents gave the first solid evidence that elements of the 1st NV A Division were attempting to infiltrate the Republic. In western Chuong Thien Province the number of enemy incidents was high, but most were minor. and friendly casualties were light.

At the beginning of June enemy activity began at a low level, rose sharply during the second and third weeks, and tapered off again. Highlights, of June enemy activity included two unsuccessful attacks on Tuyen Binh district town (Kien Tuong Province) which were probably designed to cover infiltration into Base Area 470. Elsewhere in the Delta there was only scattered enemy activity, including two attempts to overrun district towns. Reports indicated"enemy intentions to seize as much terrain as possible, to gain control of a large segment of the population, and to counter Vietnamization and pacification during the phase of the offensive beginning in July.

July 1 to September 30, 1972

During the first month of the third quarter enemy activity in Military Region 4 began at a moderate level, but declined from a high of 24 incidents per day for the first week to an average of 14 the last week. The heaviest 'concentration of activity occurred in Dinh Tuong and Kien Hoa Provinces. In early July enemy forces initiated action to seize the triborder area in the vicinity of Base Area 470. TACAIR and B-52 strikes there and around San" Giang district town forced enemy withdrawal to the west on 12 July. Throughout the rest of the Delta enemy activities were characterized by rocket and mortar attacks and light ground attacks.

In August enemy incidents were at a low level except for a moderate increase in the middle of the month. Most activity was concentrated in Dinh Tuong Province, except for the evening of 14 August when there was a series of shellings in Kien Hoa Province. Indications were that the enemy was continuing to infiltrate elements of a division as well as other units into Dinh Tuong Province. Apparent enemy targets were Route 4, district towns in western Dinh Tuong Province, My Tho City, and the Cho Cao Canal. Enemy activity during the month consisted of sporadic ground contacts, shellings, and probes apparently intended to divert friendly forces while the enemy continued the infiltration of personnel and supplies.

At the close of the third quarter enemy activity was at a moderate level, concerned primarily toward keeping open major resupply and infiltration routes. Activities were characterized by scattered rocket and mortar attacks, ground contacts, and small sapper attacks. One enemy objective in September appeared to be the establishment of a base area in the Seven Mountains area of Chau Doc Province to be used as a springboard for future activity. In VC Military Region 2 the enemy attacked government outposts which were restricting the southward movement of men and supplies into Base Area 470. In VC Military Region 3 similar activity occurred as the enemy attempted to lessen government control over supply routes and to prepare forward areas east of the U-Minh Forest leading into Chuong Thien Province

October 1 to December 30, 1972

[At the beginning of the 4th Quarter] enemy activity was at a low to moderate level. It

was characterized by attempts to interdict major land and water routes with particular emphasis

on Route 4, the main road leading from the Delta to Saigon. The enemy hoped to force ARVN

units to concentrate along the lines of communication, leaving the countryside undefended.

There were also numerous attacks-by-fire and small ground attacks against lower level

Government of Vietnam administrative centers to discredit the government and the pacification

program. Concurrently. Enemy main force units were moving into the Delta from

Cambodia in order to strengthen the enemy position prior to a cease-fire. Throughout November

enemy initiated activity continued at a low level. All available information indicated that the

enemy was continuing his attempts to infiltrate men and supplies into the Delta from Cambodia.

The limited enemy activities were aimed at securing routes from Cambodia to permit the safe

transit of critically needed food, medicine. and ammunition. Once in the Delta enemy forces

were breaking down into small units which dispersed throughout the region in order to claim as

much control as possible over the land and population prior to any cease-fire

The only enemy activity that increased in November was terrorism, which was

characterized by the selective assassination of government officials and the bombing of public

places. These acts were probably implemented to demonstrate the government's inability to

provide adequate protection, to eliminate or intimidate potential opposition. and to maintain

visibility without risk of heavy losses.

In the" first week of December enemy initiated activity increased noticeably. In VC

Military Region2 the movement of supplies south was noted, probably into Dinh Tuong

Province, where reports indicated serious shortages of mortar and rocket ammunition. In VC

Military Region 3 enemy activity was concentrated in Chuang Thien Province, typified by

attacks-by-fire and small ground attacks meant to disrupt the pacification and Vietnamization

programs while extending enemy influence prior to and during a cease-fire. Following this brief

upsurge, enemy activity declined to a low level during the remainder of the month. Intelligence

indicated that the enemy probably lacked the manpower and supplies necessary to sustain large

scale operations and would instead employ terrorism as the principal means to discredit

Government of Vietnam [efforts].

(Minor corrections made in the transcript, mainly typo error adjustments.)

APPENDIX 7

VC Taxation (Extortion) Report

CONFIDENTIAL

1601-03 *File*
(5)

IV

HEADQUARTERS
DELTA REGIONAL ASSISTANCE COMMAND
APO 96215
Office of the Deputy for CORDS

MACDR-CR-PX   26 October 1972

SUBJECT: Quarterly VC Extortion (Taxation) Summary (U)

SEE DISTRIBUTION

1. (U) Attached for information is the Quarterly VC Extortion
(Taxation) Summary for the period 1 July to 30 September 1972.

2. (C) VC progress in their preparations for a fall offensive and
cease-fire is dependent upon VC extortion efforts. Although extortion
activity increased during the quarter, results to date have not apparently been sufficient to satisfy VC needs. Information obtained from
documents, ralliers, and other sources point to a massive VC effort to
collect funds during the fourth quarter of 1972. An ultimate goal of
this effort could be the outright purchasing of positions within the
GVN organization at hamlet and village levels for a political offensive
during a possible cease-fire. Additionally, these funds could be used
to sustain a renewed offensive either prior to US elections or in the
event of a failure to obtain a settlement in the cease-fire negotiations

3. (C) Advisors in MR 4 should bring to the attention of their counterparts the contents of this Quarterly VC Extortion Summary. It is anticipated that the VC will make a maximum effort in MR 4 during the coming
rice harvest to extort funds from the people to prolong the war

WILBUR WILSON
Deputy for CORDS

1 Incl
as

DISTRIBUTION   CLASSIFIED BY DEPCORDS, MR 4
A1, B, C   SUBJECT TO GDS OF EXEC ORDER 11652
1 - MACCORDS-PH   DECLASSIFY ON 31 DECEMBER 1978
10-PSD
25-Phung-Hoang   THIS DOCUMENT IS RELEASABLE TO
                                THE REPUBLIC OF VIETNAM

CONFIDENTIAL

171

CONFIDENTIAL

HEADQUARTERS
DELTA REGIONAL ASSISTANCE COMMAND
APO 96215

Office of the Deputy for CORDS

MACDR-CR-PX

SUBJECT: Quarterly VC Extortion (Taxation) Summary (U)

1. (U) PURPOSE: To analyze the VC extortion/taxation effort in MR4,
during the third quarter of calendar year 1972.

2. (C) DISCUSSION:

    a. Pacification Research Reports and Province Extortion Reports
constituted the main content of this study and provided sufficient information on which to base an estimate of VC extortion, to include an
analysis of the methods and rates of extortion, and an evaluation of VC
uses of collections. Special reports were also used in this study to
complete the overview of VC extortion efforts in MR4. Annexes A through
F provide a detailed analysis of the extortion effort.

    b. Of primary interest during this quarter was the use of funds
resulting from VC tax collections. It has been rumored that the stated
goal of the VCI in one province is to extort maximum amounts of funds
so that they can be used in an attempt to purchase positions of key
importance; such as village or hamlet chiefs, for their cadre to fill
within the GVN organizational structure. The VC purpose of such an
effort would be to obtain an optimum vantage point for conducting VC
political campaigns during and after an agreement for a ceasefire. This
attempt comes at a critical point in time as the maneuvering for political
advantage by all concerned is designed to influence world opinion and
more importantly, those who may possibly supervise a ceasefire.

    c. Prices and rates both continued to climb during the third quarter.
Of particular interest was the increase in the market price of paddy from
800$VN per gia to 1,000$VN per gia, and the increase in the rate of extortion as reflected by the revised extortion table percentages based on per
capita rates. No economic activity or location in the Delta was immune

CLASSIFIED BY PHUNG HOANG ADVISOR, DRAC   THIS DOCUMENT IS RELEASABLE
SUBJECT GENERAL DECLASSIFICATION   TO REPUBLIC OF VIETNAM
SCHEDULE OF EXECUTIVE ORDER 11652
AUTOMATICALLY DOWNGRADED AT TWO-YEAR
INTERVALS, DECLASSIFIED ON 31 DEC 78

CONFIDENTIAL

MACDR-CR-FX
SUBJECT: Quarterly VC Extortion (Taxation) Summary (U)

from some type of increase in both prices and rates. These increases are regarded as sufficient evidence to warrant the conclusion that the VC are financially strained and do not have the funds on hand to continue the military and political struggle on the level at which they feel it must be conducted in the coming months. In addition to the rate and price increases, it was noted throughout MR4 that while collection activity increased, actual collections were probably less than during the two immediately preceding reporting periods.

d. The greater access to the population created by the spring offensive, increased VCI collection activity during the third quarter of the calendar year 1972, increased prices and rates of extortion up to 50% above previously reported levels, the stated goals of COSVN and Province Party Committees, and the onset of the harvest season beginning in November, presage unprecedented extortion activity during the fourth quarter of 1972 and during the first quarter of 1973.

3. (C) CONCLUSIONS:

a. The VC are currently engaged in using their extortion monies to ruthlessly achieve political goals in an effort to affect future political trends in MR4. The effort to entrench their cadre in key official positions at the grassroots level, through bribery and the purchase of positions, is a program that must be immediately examined. Other uses of their funds include purchasing of local supplies, feeding the troops, ransoming key VCI, and bribing government officials to allow them to operate with impunity.

b. As in the last extortion study, it is concluded that people are reluctant to report extortion incidents to GVN authorities in most provinces, and they will not report incidents in the future until they are fully reassured that no adverse effects on their personal lives will be felt, and that it is advantageous for them to report these incidents.

c. VC extortion activity will continue at a very high level during the last quarter of 1972, with results being more commensurate with effort expended as the harvest season begins in November and continues into January. All of the convergent factors mentioned in paragraph 2d will result in enough funds to pay the debts incurred by the previous offensive and to finance military and political action campaigns at levels of their own choosing unless GVN agencies continue to step up their counter-finance and economy drive. Projections, based on Province estimates of VC collections for the first three quarters of 1972, are that the VC will extort somewhat more than two billion piasters in the Delta during the calendar year.

2

CONFIDENTIAL

MACDR-CR-PX
SUBJECT: Quarterly VC Extortion (Taxation) Summary (U)

4. (C) RECOMMENDATIONS:

a. The intensive propaganda campaign which was begun during the third
quarter of 1972 should be continued and given full GVN agency support.
The aim of the campaign should be:

(1) To inform the people of how extortion money is being used by
the VC to hurt the best interests of the people.

(2) To continue to encourage the people to avoid paying VC
demands and to explain how to avoid or delay payment until GVN authorities
can be informed.

(3) To convince the population that the police will not arrest
them or prosecute them when they report extortion attempts, but will make
every effort to apprehend Finance and Economy cadre.

b. Provinces and Districts should be informed that during the fourth
quarter of 1972, neutralization of VCI Finance and Economy cadre takes
precedence over any other targeting and that the best way to obtain
results is to specifically target all such cadre.

c. Controls should be established in the payment of funds to land
owners under the Land to the Tiller program to preclude the type of extortion noted in this study in which the major portion of a large check was
contributed by a landowner as ransom for his kidnapped wife.

d. There is a great need to determine the status of all village and
hamlet chiefs who have been appointed since the institution of martial
law. A careful screening policy should be conducted within each province
to insure that VCI are not using their funds to obtain positions within
the GVN structure.

e. National Police must insure that victims reporting extortion
activity will not be arrested or prosecuted. Lengthy questioning periods can
have as deleterious an effect as actual incarceration.

ANNEXES:

A. Rates of Extortion by Types of Economic Activity (U)

B. Estimated Collections, 1 JAN - 30 SEP 72 (U)

C. VC Uses of Collections (U)

3

CONFIDENTIAL

CONFIDENTIAL

MACDR-CR-PX
SUBJECT: Quarterly VC Extortion (Taxation) Summary (U)

D. Methods of Notification and Collection of Extortion Amounts (U)

    Appendix 1 to Annex D

E. Promised Returns for Sums Extorted (U)

F. Changes Since the Second Quarter Extortion Summary (U)

4

CONFIDENTIAL

CONFIDENTIAL

ANNEX A - RATES OF EXTORTION BY TYPES OF ECONOMIC ACTIVITY (U)

1. (C) Past extortion studies have noted that for any given form of economic activity, there is a VC tax levied. In 1972, in addition to rises in the price of extortion as the market cost of rice has expanded, there have been reports of increased rates of extortion which represent an absolute increase rather than a relative one merely keeping pace with the inflation rate. In the past, while there have been some divergencies in the price of extortion, rates were based on the standard rice production table as presented in previous studies. For this study, not only was there a reported change in the rate table, but there were indications that various VC Province Committees were informed that a monumental collection effort must be made in the fall and winter with disregard to the present rate table. To accomplish the assigned mission many of the Committees have demanded that finance and economy cadre collect twice the rate which has been applied in the past. In addition to the increased rates and prices of rice special fund drives have been mounted among the people for purposes of providing funds for higher headquarters, as well as to fill local needs. There are reports, again this quarter, of exhortations to families to maintain sufficient rice on hand to feed infiltrating troops. Propaganda has also emphasized that this rice would be used to provide sustenance to NVA troops who would be in the Delta after the ceasefire.

2. (C) Although cadre in several provinces have been instructed to disregard previous extortion tables and collect as much as possible, this maxim seems to have been applied late in the third quarter and thus will carry over into the fourth quarter. Rates during the third quarter remained relatively similar throughout MR4 though variations were applied to meet local situations. VC collections can be divided into agricultural, commercial, transportation, fishing, and special purpose extortion. The economy of the Delta is based primarily on rice, and as would be expected, rice is not only the most collected commodity for an "in-kind" payment, but is also the generally applied standard on which to base other rates.

   a. Agricultural Extortion Rates:

     (1) Rice Production Rates:

      (a) Of particular interest this past quarter was the reported increased extortion rate for rice production. Since rice provides the basis for the economy of the Delta, and since the VC measure most other forms of economic endeavor against the price of paddy rice, the importance of this commodity cannot be overemphasized. Although the increase in the

A - 1

CONFIDENTIAL

CONFIDENTIAL

market price of paddy was from 800$VN to 1,000$VN per gia, a rate increase reflecting an absolute rise in the amount demanded for rice produced in the Delta is of greater significance. The following chart is extracted from a Pacification Research Report on VC Taxation in Ba Xuyen Province (Report 4/BX/17/72, dated 24 Sep 72), and represents a general increase of 5% in the extortion rate on the amount of gia of paddy produced by a farm family:

REVISED RICE PRODUCTION
EXTORTION RATE TABLE

PRODUCTION			EXTORTION RATE
FROM: 5 gia of paddy	TO:	8 gia	12% (Old rate: 7%)
9		11	13
12		14	14
15		17	15
18		20	16
21		23	17
24		26	18
27		29	19
30		32	20
33		35	21
36		38	22
39		41	23
42		44	24
45		47	25
48		50	26
51		55	28
56		60	30
61		65	32

A - 2

CONFIDENTIAL

66	70	34
71	75	36
76	80	38
81	85	40
86	90	42
91	to infinity	45 (Old rate 40%)

This table is one of three methods used to determine rice production rates. To use this table the first step is to determine total production by a family unit, divide the total by the number of persons composing the household unit, arrive at a per capita figure, refer to the extortion table to determine the percentage of extortion, and then multiply this percentage times total production. For example, assume that a family of four persons produced 300 gia of paddy on their 20 cong of riceland. The following computations would be made:

a. Determine individual income: $\frac{300 \text{ gia total production}}{4 \text{ family members}} = 75$ gia per capita

b. Find the extortion ratio on the table: 71 - 75 gia = 36% extortion rate

c. Each individual is taxed: .36 x 75 = 27 gia

d. The family has to pay 27 x 4 = 108 gia

Persons counted into the calculation, according to the PRT survey of Ke Sach District, Ba Xuyen, included those who died during the year, babies born before the establishment of the tax dossier, students who attend school in the city but are supported by their families, political prisoners arrested by the GVN, hired laborers, and wounded soldiers (included in this category are those who resisted the French, soldiers and cadre of the mainforce units, and local force guerrillas who left home and are still in the VC ranks). In addition, a wounded soldier can be counted for two allocations—one at his family and another at the family that supports him. Adjustments can be made, according to the Ke Sach PRT survey, in the case of crop failure or disaster. In these instances the following table may then be applied:

Damage attaining 21-40% of production = 35% exemption

Damage attaining 41-50% of production = 50% exemption

Damage attaining 51-60% of production = 70% exemption

A - 3

CONFIDENTIAL

Damage over 61% of production - Full exemption

In addition, a poor family working on 10 cong of riceland can be fully exempt if damage is over 50% of production. Reductions also may be given in case of scattered losses.

(2) According to a respondent in the Ba Xuyen PRT survey, "the revised extortion table was essential for supporting the VC/NVA effort on the battlefield and for making up a lack of adequate funds." It is believed that the VC are currently unable to collect the amount of funds by use of the old table and were forced to resort to a rate increase to attempt to retrieve their losses. If this is so, then this is an indication that the time is propitious to increase countermeasures against the Finance and Economy collection activity during the coming harvest season. Further severe limitations could cause further rate increases, generating dissatisfaction among the general populace as the VC demands become greater, while at the same time reaching the desired effect of causing the VC effort to "wither away".

(3) When the VC cannot estimate the quantity of rice produced, an extra two steps are added into the first process by categorizing the quality of riceland owned and determining the amount of land farmed. The procedure then becomes the same as in the first method by estimating production on a per capita basis, applying the appropriate extortion rate, and then multiplying total estimated production times the rate. Although land productivity varies from province to province with the use of fertilizers and different strains of rice, land may be rated as follows for a typical province:

A Category Land - estimated productivity is 150 gia per hectare.

B Category Land - estimated productivity is 100 gia per hectare.

C Category Land - estimated productivity is 80 gia per hectare.

This method of estimating amounts to be extorted places the farmer at a severe disadvantage when crops are lean. However, as previously shown, the VC usually make allowances for drought and crop failure.

(4) A third method is to assess a flat rate, which is often used in addition to measuring productivity. Although this is most frequently applied to poor farmers as a minimum payment level, in some provinces it is also applied to all lands as a supplement to other forms of extortion. The usual minimum level that must be paid by a poor farmer is 2,000$VN and the flat rate can be set as high as 50,000$VN per hectare under cultivation. For orchard land, it may be as much as 30,000$VN.

(2) _Tractor Extortion._ The usual method of determining the amount to be collected from tractor owners is to charge an annual flat sum.

A - 4

CONFIDENTIAL

179

CONFIDENTIAL

In the past this amount had been reported to be up to 50,000$VN. Province reports for the third quarter showed the cost to be as high as 160,000$VN for a large tractor in Vinh Binh. Ba Xuyen and Chau Doc Provinces both reported a new average tractor rate of 100,000$VN per annum. A second method of computation is to estimate the net income of a tractor owner and apply a scale of from 20 - 40% of the profit realized on sales of commodities produced on tractor cultivated acreage. A third way is to charge a rate on cultivation of land based on acreage plowed by the tractor owner regardless of the sale of produce. Special fines are sometimes levied on those who use tractors to plow land laying fallow. Presumably these fines are imposed because complete cultivation of the Delta would serve to reduce maneuverable areas for the VC.

(3) Extortion of certain minor crops is also lucrative for the VC depending on the prevalence of the crop in a local area.

(a) In Kien Giang, for example, several of these minor crops together constitute the major share of agricultural extortion collected during the third quarter. Pineapples are charged the cash equivalent of 17 gia of rice per 1/10 Ha, peppers are 1500 - 2500$VN per plant, or 350$VN per kg of dried pepper. Sweet potatoes are charged according to garden size:

From 1 to 5 cong	2,000$VN
From 5 to 10 cong	5,000$VN
From 10 to 15 cong	8,000$VN
From 15 to 20 cong	10,000$VN

In addition, vegetable gardens are charged from 15,000 to 30,000$VN per Ha, according to land quality; and coconut and sugar cane are estimated to be 10% of market value.

(b) Some sample rates placed on other minor crops are as follows:

Hac Nua (CD)	9$VN per kilo
Corn (CD)	9$VN per kilo
Lychee Nuts (BL)	30% of gross income
Water Buffalo (BL. CT)	200$VN ea or 30% of sale price
Hogs (BL)	5$VN per kilo
Chickens and Ducks	30$VN per year

A - 5

CONFIDENTIAL

b. <u>Commerical Extortion Rates.</u> This form of extortion while not approaching the total yield of agricultural extortion often results in quick and large returns for the VC coffers. VC succeed in extorting money from commercial ventures due to the vulnerability of the physical assets of the entrepreneur. Even in larger cities, the businessman's investment is still subject to reprisals if an extortion demand is not met. The businessman thus often has little alternative between paying demands or being put out of business. Under these circumstances such costs must be considered a part of doing business and the consumer eventually pays the increased price of goods or services.

(1) As with agricultural extortion, commerical rates vary from province to province. The amounts reportedly demanded from commercial enterprises have doubled throughout MR4 since the second quarter report. Some current examples of average extortion demands follows with ranges noted. Range is based on size, wealth, location and productivity.

Enterprise	Annual Range Extortion	Average Annual Rate of Extortion
Rice Mill	20,000 - 500,000$VN	200,000$VN
Saw Mill		100,000$VN
Sampan Factory	30,000 - 300,000$VN	200,000$VN
Brick Kiln	50,000 - 300,000$VN	150,000$VN
Ice Plant	50,000 - 300,000$VN	200,000$VN
Nuoc Mam Plant		30,000$VN
Grocery Store	10,000 - 200,000$VN	25,000$VN
Pharmacy	2,000 - 15,000$VN	10,000$VN
Restaurant/Cafes		15,000$VN
Movie Theaters		25,000$VN
Hotels		25,000$VN
Textile Retail Stores		15,000$VN
Textile Factory		20,000$VN
Hardware/Electrical Shop		15,000$VN
Tailor Shop		15,000$VN

4 - 6

CONFIDENTIAL

Barber Shop	10,000$VN
Radio/TV Shop	20,000$VN
Motorcycle Repair Shop	15,000$VN
Motorcycle Dealer	25,000$VN
Gasoline Station	30,000$VN
Shoe Store	10,000$VN
Hand Craft	5,000$VN
Gold Dealer	20,000$VN
Rock Quarry	50,000 - 75,000$VN	65,000$VN
Lime Kiln	20,000 - 30,000$VN	25,000$VN

(2) The following generalizations can be made from this chart: First, the extortion amount for the major industries and means of production are extensive. When one takes a province such as Ba Xuyen and notes the tax potential, as shown below, one can see the vast amounts that can be collected by selectively extorting major industrial concerns.

Ba Xuyen Enterprises

Concern	Number	Average Annual Rate of Extortion	Annual Extortion Potential
Saw Mill	10	100,000$VN	1,000,000$VN
Rice Mill	185	200,000$VN	37,000,000$VN
Brick Kiln	7	150,000$VN	1,050,000$VN
Ice Plant	7	200,000$VN	1,400,000$VN
Sampan Factory	52	200,000$VN	10,400,000$VN
		TOTAL	50,850,000$VN

Second, small shop keepers must pay between 10,000$VN and 30,000$VN. While those who operate the major enterprises may be able to rebuild their concern if damaged, the small shopkeeper is more subject to pressure because it may take a much longer time for him to build up working capital again should his business be destroyed.

A - 7

CONFIDENTIAL

c. <u>Transportation Extortion Rates</u>. Transportation vehicles such as barges, water taxis and sampans are highly susceptible to VC threats because of the need to traverse VC infested areas of MR4 either to go to market or to return home from market. Some sample extortion rates on transportation are as follows:

Mode of Transport	Range of Rates	Average Annual Rate
Three wheel lambretta	1,000 - 20,000$VN	10,000$VN
Motorized Sampan	500$VN	10,000$VN
Bus	5,000 - 20,000$VN	10,000$VN
Truck	10,000 - 25,000$VN	15,000$VN
Water Taxi	3,000 - 12,000$VN	10,000$VN
Barge	30 - 40% of income	30 - 40% income

The normal method of extracting sums from drivers of motorized vehicles is to establish a mobile checkpoint along a canal or roadway and stop vehicles coming through the gauntlet. Extortion can be by the year, by the load, by the number of passengers, or by the amount of assessed income. It also may be a combination of several of these methods. Owners of bus companies, cyclos, or several sampans may be subjected to a tax of up to 50% of estimated profit. But reports were not available to substantiate specific rates on vehicles or extortion of owners of transportation companies.

d. <u>Fishing Industry Extortion</u>. As with extortion on agricultural produce, commercial enterprises, and transportation vehicles; so the rates on pisciculture have also expanded in 1972. Among the fishing activities taxed by the VC are fish ponds, fishing rights, fish traps and amount of fish caught. Following are some current representative rates:

Fishing Activity	Annual Rate
Fishing rights	20,000 - 50,000$VN
Occupational fee (license)	10,000 - 50,000$VN
Fish traps	15,000 - 25,000$VN
Fish ponds	5,000 - 10,000$VN

It was estimated that in the third quarter of CY 72, collections on fishing rights alone in Chau Doc Province were 15,340,000$VN. This is no small industry.

A - 8

e. Special Purpose Extortion. This form of extortion is designed to suppress an economic activity which is inimical to VC designs, rather than just the collection of sums of money. The following examples fit this category:

(1) PSDF Levy. This levy which is designed more to discourage families from letting their sons be PSDF members than to extort major sums of money, was noted in Kien Phong Province during the second quarter and in Kien Tuong Province during the third quarter. The rate is 1,000$VN for each PSDF member.

(2) Dog Fine. A dog tax was reported for the second quarter in Kien Hoa. Even though a payment was made, the dog was usually killed by the VC. During the third quarter, a similar levy was reported in Chuong Thien, Kien Tuong and Phong Dinh. The rate is from 1,000 - 2,000$VN per dog. In Chuong Thien, this fine was particularly prevalent when dogs were kept near GVN outposts. This tax is apparently thus designed to discourage dog ownership rather than to collect the cash alone. The reason is that dogs give warnings of night intruders or can expose guerrilla movements.

(3) Forest Use Levy. During the second quarter it was reported in Vinh Binh Province that an assessment of 5,000$VN was made when trees or shrubs were cut. Again discouragement of an activity which might endanger a VC position seemed to be the motivation for the fine.

(4) Association Dues. This was a special purpose assessment of 565$VN per member of the VC Can Tho Province Farmer's Association.

f. Additional Extortion Rates:

(1) "In-kind" extortion is used to provide food for infiltrating enemy troops or to feed local guerrillas, as well as to acquire materials that may otherwise be difficult to purchase or awkward to carry. Of course, when a family does not have the cash on hand that the VC are demanding, then the VC may elect the option of accepting payment in the bulk commodity. A partial listing of bulk commodities demanded during the third quarter includes: dried fish, rice, shrimp, salt, bread, canned meats, nails, gasoline and oil products, and wood.

(2) Fund drives have been the fashion during the third quarter for almost all provinces within MR4. According to a PRT survey conducted in Vinh Long, VC extortion activities increased during the third quarter in the form of a fund drive. Respondents stated that the people who paid during the first and second quarters were revisited by the VC in the third quarter as well. The VC asked for 3,000$VN from poor families, 5,000 - 7,000$VN from richer families. The VC explained, "The Liberation Front needs money very much; (therefore), people should try to help them." A 47

A - 9

,ear old respondent added that he had paid 15,000$VN in March, and was
very unhappy because the VC returned in September to ask for 7,000$VN in
addition to the original amount. A respondent to a PRT survey in Ba Xuyen
Province stated, "In accordance with COSVN Instruction #15, taxation
increases are to support the battlefield and make up a lack of finances.
This taxation aims at draining all the 1971 unpaid taxes, and in addition,
making a fund drive (among people who have already paid their due) in
which they have to donate from 10,000 - 100,000$VN." Most of the provinces
reported a troop support tax during the quarter of at least 1,000$VN per
family.

(3) A house tax is another form of property tax with valuation of
wealth of the owner determining the amount demanded. In Kien Tuong and
Kien Hoa Provinces, extortion for housing was from 500 - 5,000$VN. The
Kien Hoa tax rate was applied as follows:

Poor farmer	500$VN per year
Average farmer	5,000$VN per year
Private property owner	1,000$VN per year
Landlord	3,000$VN per year

In Vinh Chau District of Bac Lieu Province, the range was from 5,000$VN to
15,000$VN per year. The housing tax is often an additional fee which is
added on to the tax for the land which also may be owned by the same family

(4) A head tax was noted in several reports. In Chau Doc, a head
tax totalling 7,000$VN per family unit was charged in the third quarter of
1972. In Kien Hoa, it was called a personal tax and ranged from 200$VN
to 1,000$VN per person.

(5) There are other miscellaneous taxes levied against produce,
goods, and services in the Delta. Among those mentioned in past studies
are exports from VC controlled areas and imports into those areas. Import
and export extortions can range from no tax to 100% of the original cost
if it is felt the product is either a special luxury, or is dangerous to
the VC interests. Some items such as GVN newspapers and magazines are
usually confiscated at VC checkpoints and later destroyed. The following
examples of current "export/import" taxes were provided in a PRT report on
Ba Xuyen Province:

(a) Exit tax (on goods from a VC controlled area going to the
city): 15% on rice, 10% on fruit, 15% on pigs, and 20% on poultry. All
commodities, except rice are free of duty if personally taken to market by
the producer.

A - 10

CONFIDENTIAL

(b) Entry tax (goods leaving the city and going to VC controlled areas): strong wine, luxury articles, cigarettes, and nylon material are levied from 50 - 100% of cost. Light wine is levied 20% of cost and canned food is levied 35% of cost.

It was reported that abductions of wealthy people for ransom have proven particularly lucrative in Kien Hoa Province. The VC are targeting land owners receiving compensation under the Land to the Tiller Program (LTTT) law. A former landlord living in Giong Trom District, Kien Hoa, received a check from the LTTT program in the amount of 674,000$VN on 10 September 1972. On 18 September, four VC in ARVN 7th Division uniforms knocked on his door and kidnapped his wife. The next day an elderly lady brought a letter to him with the hammer and sickle seal on it demanding 406,000$VN for the release of his wife. On 25 September, he cashed the check, paid the money to the lady, and his wife was returned that same night. On September 26, this incident was reported to the police. This is one of two terrorist incidents involving LTTT payments in Giong Trom District reported during the month of September. If this extortion practice is widespread throughout the Delta, a few carefully selected targets can help meet all VC collection goals in a given district with relative ease.

(6) It can be seen from the foregoing analysis that if there is a product in existence or a service that can be performed, the VC will make every effort to tax it. Thus a commodity that is being produced may be subject to successive extortions. For example, the commodity may be taxed at its point of origin, subjected to tax on the way to market - the person providing the transportation service also being taxed in the process, and if a purchase is made or trade concluded, not only will there be a rakeoff at the market, but the new goods will be taxed on the way home. This massive amount of double and triple taxing contributes to the creeping inflation in the GVN system. The costs of paying extortion sums are passed on to the consumer in the form of higher prices.

A - 11

CONFIDENTIAL

CONFIDENTIAL

ANNEX B - ESTIMATED COLLECTIONS, 1 JAN - 30 SEP 1972 (U)

1. (C) Estimates for the third quarter of CY 72 varied considerably
from province to province making generalization of trends impractical.
For example, in Vinh Long, where 13,344,300$VN had been reported as
being collected for the first half of 1972, the amount for the third
quarter was 14,783,616$VN thus surpassing in three months the total for
six months. The fact that from 65 - 80% of collections are normally
made during the first few months of the year points out how low the estimate was for the first two quarters of 1972. It was stated in the Vinh
Long report that the increase shown for the third quarter was due to improved information and analysis. Similarly, an excellent analysis provided by Chau Doc for VC An Giang Province (GVN Chau Doc plus An Giang
Province), set the third quarter collections at 77,136,000$VN. This
figure is also more than the combined first six-month total estimated at
71,110,000$VN. Estimates for An Xuyen were more than 4,000,000$VN above
the reported amount for the previous quarter. At the other extreme was
Vinh Binh, which reported collections for the first six months to be
172,000,000$VN, and for the third quarter as 18,150,000$VN. This data
reported by Vinh Binh is suspect, since it runs counter to reports from
all other provinces. No estimates were provided by Kien Phong, Kien
Tuong, or Sa Dec.

2. (C) Since there were such widely divergent estimates from province
to province, and since some provinces reported no estimates while others
left the question open to further speculation, the chart in the next paragraph is a composite of several methods of analysis. The method used was
dependent on the types of information provided by each province. When a
province estimate was given (usually based on information or estimates by
each district) that figure served as the best estimate for the third
quarter. This was true in the cases of An Xuyen, Chau Doc and An Giang,
Phong Dinh, Bac Lieu, Chuong Thien, Vinh Binh and Vinh Long. In those
cases, no attempt was made to change the amount provided. Where no estimates were provided (Kien Phong, Kien Tuong, and Sa Dec), a best estimate
was derived through a comparison with percentages collected for a similar
time frame in 1971, with the probable amount collected as a percentage of
that which was collected for the first six months, and with whatever frag-
mentary evidence was available. Al of Go Cong's collections were documented ones, so the estimate could range much higher than shown here.
Although considerable information was provided by most of the other provinces, an estimate was not pinpointed. A case in point is Kien Giang,
where extensive analysis was provided. In the report it said 113,000,000
$VN was the official estimate for 1 Jan - 30 Jul. Since 85,000,000$VN

B-1

CONFIDENTIAL

CONFIDENTIAL

was estimated for the first six months through 30 June, subtraction produced 28,000,000$VN for the month of July. Considering a probable drop in collection during the growing season and a reduction in fishing activity during August and September, an additional (very conservative) 17,000,000$VN was added to these two months producing a total of 45,000,000 $VN for the third quarter estimate. Similar arithmetic methods were applied on the remaining provinces as needed.

3. (C) A note of caution should be added. First, as stated in the second Quarterly Report for CY 72, the estimates for the period of January through 30 June, were regarded as basically low. For purposes of statistical additivity, continuity, and because statements were often made in reports submitted by provinces that previous reports were far too conservative, it was determined there was insufficient information to make a totally revised estimate for the year to date. Therefore, a reconciliation of figures should be made at the end of the current calendar year based on the total information available. Second, where province estimates were provided which were based on good intelligence collection and analysis, estimates tended to be more realistic during the third quarter. Thus while a report from a province may state that activity increased and collections decreased compared to the previous quarter, there is no real contradiction if the sum estimated for the third quarter approaches or matches that recorded as the total for the first six months. Third, the estimates also generally reflect a price of paddy increase from 800$VN to 1,000$VN. In most of the provinces, collection demands have been raised double the amount requested in 1971. Part of the increase is due to inflation, but rates as well as prices have increased as was pointed out in Annex A. A chart of estimated VC collections during the third quarter of CY 72 follows:

ESTIMATES OF TOTAL VC COLLECTIONS (1 JAN TO 30 SEP 72)

Province	Estimate for 1st six months	Estimate for Third Quarter	Total Estimate 1 Jan to 30 Sep
An Xuyen	36,170,000$VN	27,450,000$VN	63,620,000$VN
Bac Lieu	22,604,000	85,916,600	108,520,600
Ba Xuyen	84,000,000	51,600,000	135,600,000
Chau Doc/An Giang	71,110,000	77,136,000	148,246,000
Chuong Thien	20,760,000	150,000,000	170,760,000
Dinh Tuong	117,900,000	40,000,000	157,900,000
Go Cong	63,000	477,000	540,000

B-2

CONFIDENTIAL

Province	Estimate for 1st six months	Estimate for Third Quarter	Total Estimate 1 Jan to 30 Sep
Kien Giang	85,000,000	45,000,000	130,000,000
Kien Hoa	90,260,000	63,645,628	153,905,628
Kien Phong	40,000,000	5,000,000	45,000,000
Kien Tuong	11,000,000	4,000,000	15,000,000
Phong Dinh	100,000,000	43,000,000	143,000,000
Sa Dec	2,000,000	500,000	2,500,000
Vinh Binh	172,000,000	18,150,000	190,150,000
Vinh Long	13,344,300	14,783,616	28,127,916
	866,211,300$VN	626,658,844$VN	1,492,870,144$VN

4. (C) It has been stated in previous studies that VC collections are
conservatively biased by officials and analysts alike. Several studies
this quarter used some excellent analytical devices, which while conservatively biased, produced some dramatic differences in the estimate of
possible VC extortion in MR4. If these independent analyses are indicative
of the bias put into previous reports, extortion could range from 4 to 6
times that recorded by some of the provinces in the past.

B-3

● CONFIDENTIAL ●

ANNEX C - VC USES OF COLLECTIONS (U)

1. (C) It is known that the extortion effort in MR4 is largely responsible for sustaining not only the VCI and the NVA within the Delta, but it is also responsible for the sustenance of units outside of MR4, including COSVN and troops fighting in the North and Central Highlands. However, reports of more insidious uses than simple support of combatants are becoming increasingly common. In addition to supporting troops with supplies, medicines, and money, the extortion effort in MR4 is being used internally to buy GVN positions from officials to entrench VC legal cadre for the possible ceasefire, to pay for VC immunity from investigation, to purchase an exit from captivity for high-ranking VCI, and to pay for informants and penetration agent operations conducted against ARVN and the GVN.

2. (C) Perhaps one of the most critical applications of VC funds is to purchase a position within the GVN organizational structure. This has probably been used to some extent in the past, but as the VC/NVA prepare for a possible eventual ceasefire, apparently renewed efforts are being made to purchase key positions that can be used to control portions of the Delta. Recently at a meeting held by the VC Tra Vinh Province Committee, cadre were told that VC District Committees are to identify and report all vacant hamlet chief positions in GVN-controlled hamlets. According to the source, who reported the results of the meeting, it was stated that since the martial law decree, several hamlet chiefs had been thrown out of office. According to the same report, corrupt District Chiefs are willing to replace each deposed hamlet chief with the person able to pay the largest amount of money for the vacant position and that the Province Party Committee was going to spend a large amount of money in an effort to obtain as many positions for legal cadre and VC sympathizers as can possibly be purchased. It was added that when a ceasefire occurs, hamlet chiefs under VC control would be in an excellent position to operate on behalf of the Province Committee without interference from GVN authorities. Instructions were given to launch a new tax collection program to raise funds to conduct a political action campaign in response to instructions from COSVN. Furthermore, it was stated that a COSVN order directs Province Committees to place as many legal cadre as possible in GVN positions prior to a ceasefire.

3. (C) Payment for VC immunity from investigation takes many forms including a straightforward bribe of a hamlet official or payment for allowing a vehicle through a checkpoint which is carrying supplies or VC agents. It has been reported in the past, for example, that at many police checkpoints, a few hundred piasters can insure passage without

C-1

CONFIDENTIAL

search. Other reports have noted that VC have purchased legal ID cards or identification papers from the police and have used these to conduct their subversive activities.

4. (C) Some Province Committees have a fund set aside to pay for the release of key individuals who are incarcerated by the National Police. Payments may be made to one key GVN official or may be passed around to several officials to obtain favorable results. No one is immune from the offer of such a bribe including District Chiefs, police personnel, or members of Province Security Committees. In the past, some PSCs, for example, did not classify a VCI by level (A, B, or C) until after a meeting. Thus a bribe could be used to reduce a sentence to a few months, or else to provide for an immediate release.

5. (C) Just as the GVN conducts penetration operations against the VCI, so the VCI conducts penetration operations against the GVN. Payments for information may be made either to zealous cadre, sympathizers, or to any common person who may reveal some important plan or policy. The expenses incurred by cadre are usually provided. For example, reports have shown that often agents are to wear clothing similar to that worn by the people with whom they must work, and they are given money to do this. Travel money may also be provided.

6. (C) The most prevalent use of extortion money is to pay insurgents and to supply them with foodstuffs and medicines.

    a. The task of providing for a full-time member of the VCI, VGN guerrillas, local force combatants, main force, and NVA units involves a major expenditure of funds. The following information was recorded in the Extortion Summary for the first quarter of 1972. This information, which was extracted from a document of the VC Vinh Long Province Party Committee, outlines the following authorizations for an individual for one year (1971):

Rice (paddy rice equivalent)	15 gia per year	10,500$VN
Food Allowance	3$VN per day	1,095$VN
Cloth	Four meters	800$VN
Work clothes		400$VN
Cash Allowance	100$VN per month	1,200$VN
Miscellaneous		650$VN
Total		14,645$VN

C-2

CONFIDENTIAL

This cost has now risen by at least 5,000$VN per year as a result of the increased price of paddy. Thus the amount needed to sustain one VC person may be calculated at approximately 20,000$VN per year. If one considers that there are more than 50,000 VC/NVA personnel in the Delta (this figure includes approximately 23,000 combatants as reported in DRAC PERINTREP 11-72, approximately 20,000 VCI according to the September HES rating, and at least 7,000 administrative support services troops and guerrillas as delineated in DRAC ECOINTREP 6-72), the local drain on resources for 1972 would come to approximately one billion piasters. This sum does not include their pay which comes from higher headquarters.

c. Additional expenditures are made for operating costs. Operating expenses are the normal day-to-day expenses of any bureaucratic organization to include office supplies and equipment, POL and chemicals, paper and ink for leaflets, repair parts, batteries, raw materials for production units, and payments for information. As shown in the Extortion Summary for the first quarter of CY 72, the budget for one village in VC Ben Tre Province was 86,400$VN. A listing of expenditures included office supplies, military proselyting, signal, POL and chemicals, war, medical instruments, installations, workshops, and commo-liaison.

7. (C) In past years, as much as two-thirds of collections were sent to higher headquarters where expenses for operations, troop payments, and supplies were considerable. In 1972, the problem has become even more acute as payment for the 1972 offensive and requirements for support of the drive in other parts of Vietnam and locations external to MR4, have placed strains on the VC apparatus to supply more funds. In early October, the VC Vinh Long Current Affairs Committee ordered military and political cadre to increase collections without regard to the tax scale which had been in effect for the past several years. Furthermore, COSVN suspended financial support to VC Vinh Long Province, thus forcing the Province Committee to support all VC/NVA activities within its borders except payment to military cadre. This may indicate a basic problem of meeting financial needs, a further preparation for a ceasefire and a reliance on the supplies of rice that district and village families have been requested to maintain in reserve, a change in strategy, or it could be a plan to make each Province Committee autonomous and able to function without COSVN direction. For whatever reason, an apparent new drive is underway to collect enough funds to become self-sufficient. Presumably, funds are also expected to be sent to higher headquarters for the remainder of the year.

C-3

CONFIDENTIAL

CONFIDENTIAL

ANNEX D - METHODS OF NOTIFICATION AND COLLECTION OF EXTORTION AMOUNTS (U)

1. (C) It is clear from Pacification Research Surveys and Province
Reports that VC extortion is not just a phenomenon of the peripheral
areas of the provinces or the insecure areas, but rather it is ubiquitous
and daily. While extortion is evidently reduced to a manageable minimum
in the secure areas of MR4, examples may be cited of extortion incidents
within 500 meters of an OB or of collections made within the market
places of major cities. Collections in all these areas are possible
because of differences in methods used by the VC to obtain their ends.

2. (C) The method used to notify a victim that he has a payment due to
the VC in a secure area is to use either VC underground economy and
finance cadre to notify him, or to send a relative with a note requesting
payment. When the VC legal cadre are used in this fashion, they are
vulnerable to police detection at either end of the communications
process, i.e., when they pick up the note from the VC cadre, or when they
deliver the message. The deliverance of such messages are as much of a
crime as the demand placed by the originating cadre. (See Appendix 1
to this Annex for an example of a letter sent to an intended victim.)
When the VC send a relative with a note requesting payment, they have
usually prepared for the possibility of discovery by including as part
of the request the fact that someone dear to the relative is being held
in ransom for the full payment and dire consequences are intimated for
non-compliance. Given the extended family system in Vietnam this method
is used with great frequency and achieves favorable results. Another
method of notification is to begin a whispering campaign that someone
owes a certain amount and then the person must have the proper cash ready
when the VC contact him. According to a Pacification Research Survey
conducted in Kien Phong during September, seven respondents stated that
"The VC often send a letter through the tax payer's relatives who are
government officials. This is to avoid being watched or followed up.
In case the action is discovered, the GVN will prosecute the GVN people."
According to another Pacification Research Survey conducted in Vinh Binh,
"Recently a woman merchant living in Phung Thanh Village received a
letter from the VC in which she was requested to pay 10,000$VN for two
year's tax. This woman then contacted local government officials about
this action, but the local officials did not pay attention because they
also were afraid that their lives could be threatened, though this woman's
house is located 50 meters from the public office." Past extortion
studies have also noted such incidents as legal cadre posing as traders
in markets within the province towns, so that payments can be collected
from merchants. The collection process is similar to the notification
process in that either a legal cadre or relative may be designated to

CLASSIFIED BY PHUNG HOANG ADVISOR, DRAC
SUBJECT GENERAL DECLASSIFICATION
SCHEDULE OF EXECUTIVE ORDER 11652
AUTOMATICALLY DOWNGRADED AT TWO-YEAR
INTERVALS, DECLASSIFIED ON 31 DEC 78

D-1

CONFIDENTIAL

CONFIDENTIAL

collect the funds. Alternately, the extortion victim may be required to
travel outside the secure area to a designated location to pay the full
amount of extortion. When this is done, sometimes the victim is then
forced to go with the VC to reeducation classes or to indoctrination
sessions. A 49 year old public servant in Vinh Binh reported to the PRT
that in the GVN controlled area, the VC instruct a number of businessmen
and proprietors to contribute money together. If the police learn of
this action, they are told this money is a collective fund for business
improvements. Thus the GVN has no grounds for arrest. This respondent
added that when the VC cannot make an immediate collection from someone
they temporarily disregard him. If he is later caught, then he will be
forced to pay back taxes for many years. Further refusal to pay means
death. All of the approaches noted within the previous Quarterly Extortion
Study may be used to persuade the people in secure areas to make their
payments. Thus terrorist damage may be threatened to a merchant's business.
Indirect approaches may be used to notify the person of amounts due,
direct confrontation may then be used in the collection process as a means
of emphasizing VC presence, and revisitations or renotifications may be
made if the sums do not meet the amount demanded.

3. (C) The method of notification and collection in semi-secure areas
may be a simultaneous process in which demands are levied and returns
expected within a few minutes time. The visit to a hamlet or village
may be preceded by a notification of a general time frame within which
the VC may be expected. Then the Finance and Economy cadre enter the
collection area with several armed escorts expecting payments to be ready
upon their arrival. Variations of this method are used. For example,
an indoctrination class may be held in a hamlet by a Finance and Economy
cadre, then either someone is selected to make collections and bring the
amounts to the VC at a time and place so designated, or else, time permit-
ting, collections are made on the spot with special praise given to those
who pay their full amount quickly and cheerfully. Sometimes selected VC
legal cadre are designated to make full payments enthusiastically in order
to stimulate the local population to make their payments. If groups of
people prove to be recalcitrant in the semi-secure areas, a person or
persons may be abducted and held for ransom until complete payment is
made. Selective murders are often sufficient to convince an entire
hamlet to pay immediately. In a PRT survey conducted in Ke Sach District,
Ba Xuyen, 36 respondents stated that VC extortion activities increased
in the third quarter of 1972, because village officials were assassinated
as pressure for more effective collections. As one official of Song
Phung Village put it, "On 13 August 1972, the VC disguised as National
Police conducting draft dodger operations (entered the village) in order
to assassinate the Deputy Village Council Chairman and to collect tax from
a lot of people living in the hamlet. In late (sic) July successive
assassination of village officials and hamlet chiefs occured at An My,
Ari Phung and Nhi My hamlets. The VC created pressure to make their ta-

D-2

CONFIDENTIAL

collection more effective." Obstinate taxpayers are often taken to reeducation or indoctrination sessions in VC safe areas. Several reports have also been noted of a VC unit taking someone's relative to a location where possible air strikes may be conducted by allied planes. Word of these actions create a sense of urgency which is conveyed to the person who must pay the ransom. The VC usually give receipts immediately and promise the people that they will be valid for future reference. Reports have indicated, however, that recently some VC guerrilla collection units are not giving receipts. In Kien Phong it was stated that the VC come to the person's home at night to request taxes. Those who did not have the money available were told that the VC would return on a certain time. Sometimes, the VC gathered the people in groups of 5-10 families to deliver their propaganda speeches. Much can be done in the semi-secure areas to counter the VC finance and economy drive. Penetrants into the VC apparatus can be used to determine the expected times of collection activity. If the People's Intelligence Net (PIN) is functioning properly, the location of the indoctrination session and times and expected dates of revisitation can all be identified. Specific targeting and pattern analysis can also be used to prepare operations and ambushes against the VC tax collectors.

4. (C) The process of collection is simplified in VC-controlled areas. A tax assessment is made by conducting a complete inventory of property. There are probably few who refuse to pay all taxes levied against them in these areas. If they cannot pay, then a bargaining process may reduce the amount that is demanded. Straightforward collections are made in these areas by day as well as by night. Since GVN security forces are not in evidence, little can be done in these areas until GVN control can be reestablished.

5. (C) An interesting sidelight on the collection effort was provided in a Pacification Research Team report on Ba Xuyen. A 45 year old respondent said that the VC no longer can tightly control tax collections as was the case before because they have insufficient cadre. Thus the VC cadre may take liberties to reduce the extortion assessment on paper and embezzle the rest of the funds that can be collected from the victims. This situation allegedly caused the VC Village, District and Province Party Committees to be lacking in funds while VC hamlet chiefs were becoming progressively richer. An example to support this was given in a PRT report that in Dia Chuoi Hamlet, Hoa Binh Village, Bac Lieu Province, a VC hamlet chief who recently died, left behind a large amount of money for his wife and children.

D-3

CONFIDENTIAL

APPENDIX 1 TO ANNEX D

TO: Mr. LE

At the present time, the Vietnamese fighting is stepping into a new phase that will completely destroy the Vietnamisation plan which the American Imperialists have initiated in the last invasion policy by Nixon. Thieu and the Americans are evil and crafty, they have made trouble and unhappiness for the Vietnamese people and each Vietnamese family.

The Vietnam Nation is a country of the Vietnamese. That is the never changing truth. For that reason, when the Nation and people lose their freedom and independence to the Americans, the loyal people have a duty, and responsibility to contribute to the fight against the Americans. If everybody does so, the VC people could take back and restore the Nation and save their lives from American Imperialists.

Thieu and the Americans have failed clearly in many places. The Vietnamese people could push the evil Americans out of our country, because the VN people have already selected and believe in the good cause and are supported by the people of the world, including the progressive Americans.

In the National situation, why don't you think that the VN people have sacrificed much blood and property in exchange for true freedom? Why are you not affected by the people's victimization?

I could not say all that I feel in this letter to you. So I promise that I will discuss this with you when we meet each other. Therefore, in this letter, I am only discussing your duties and responsibilities to pay the land tax to support the troops.

You have not paid the land tax for two years (last and this year). As you know the payment of the land tax is an honor, duty and political right. Now, we are temporarily charging 60 gia for each year, a total of 120 gia, worth 108,000$. We think you must perform your duty.

You may divide the payment, but first must pay 60 gia, for last year (54,000$). You may hand your money to the person who transferred this letter to you, or I will come to your family.

                    Sincerely defeat Americans
                    on 19 May 1972
                    Representative of Tay Yen F&E Section
                    5 NGHIA

          D-1-1

CONFIDENTIAL

CONFIDENTIAL

ANNEX E - PROMISED RETURNS FOR SUMS EXTORTED (U)

1. (C) It was stated in the Extortion Summary for the second quarter, that in those locations where the VC have made concrete promises that are to be fulfilled within relatively short periods of time, the GVN can exploit VC failure to live up to those promises. One question thus submitted to the Pacification Research Teams concerned those promises which the VC had made to the population of MR4. The results of these surveys showed that the VC promised little in the way of concrete benefits, and that the VC have resorted to the tactic of "borrowing" with increasing frequency.

2. (C) The VC promise few concrete benefits that will accrue to the people. For example, there are no public works promised to the population. When the VC destroy public facilities and utilities, the people become alienated because they know that the VC will not replace them. They consider their lives are made more difficult for no apparent reason. In place of promises there are either propaganda speeches or threats or violence if demands do not engender compliance. According to a PRT survey in Bac Lieu Province, in the less secure areas, the VC have promised they would use some of the money extorted from the people to repair the houses damaged by GVN artillery and air bombings. As one rallier respondent; however, stated, he had appealed to the people to support the Front when he was a VC cadre (Cell Leader, Farmer's Association Section), but when his own house was destroyed by a bomb, he received no help from the VC. Thus, he concluded that the VC only make promises, but never fulfill them. In some provinces, the tactic is to promise that willingness to pay taxes will result in a prominent post either in one of the associations, or in the eventual political structure of Vietnam in the future. Praise for being a model family is another tactic used to make a person feel he has done something important.

3. (C) Although concrete benefits are not being promised to the people, there have been increasing uses of borrowing noted in the provinces. Borrowing from the population in the form of loans has had the built-in promise of repayment after a specified period of time. Reports from various sources have placed this time frame from three to five years for loans procured during 1972. Some of the loans carry an interest note with them and almost always a receipt is given to the people with the indication that it is redeemable in the future. Many of the province reports noted that the people often burned these promisory notes because they were afraid GVN officials might find them among their personal effects. In one VC district in Vinh Long, a program of loans had recently

CLASSIFIED BY PHUNG HOANG ADVISOR, DRAC
SUBJECT GENERAL DECLASSIFICATION
SCHEDULE OF EXECUTIVE ORDER 11652
AUTOMATICALLY DOWNGRADED AT TWO-YEAR
INTERVALS, DECLASSIFIED ON 31 DEC 78

E-1

CONFIDENTIAL

been instituted because collections only reached a reported 30% of the yearly quota during the first six months of 1972. Similarly, in Ba Xuyen Province, a PRT reported that the amount of loan depended on the financial status of individuals. Five years later, the Revolutionary Government is to repay the loan. This renewed drive for funds began in July and is an additional extortion ploy supplementary to normal extortion levies. In Dinh Tuong, an additional special drive began in September to make families lend ten liters of sticky (glutinous) rice each month. The VC have promised to repay the cost of rice contributed when peace is restored.

E-2

ANNEX F - CHANGES SINCE THE SECOND QUARTER EXTORTION SUMMARY (U)

1. (C) This extortion study is a continuation of a series of quarterly reports and represents a logical progression of information, intelligence, analysis, and predictive capability. The changes which have been the most apparent may be categorized as increased activity (and demands), increased prices, increased rates, and differences in the propaganda approaches in some of the provinces.

a. Increased activity. Almost every province report stated that there had been a vast increase in extortion activity for the third quarter. It had been hypothesized in the Quarterly Extortion Summary, dated 29 July 1972, that the period from 1 July to 30 September would be characterized by a quantum increase in Finance and Economy cadre activity to attempt to pay for the losses incurred by the spring offensive and to generate sufficient funds to make an additional drive in the late fall. Most province reports seemed to be in further agreement that this increase in collection activity during the third quarter did not obtain the desired results. Many of the provinces reported that results were running between 20 - 30% below that achieved during the second quarter. This is to be expected for several reasons. First, the summer months are historically periods of low collections and the people were thus less prepared to pay even minimal demands let alone the increased demands. Second, the months of July - October are growing months in which most of the capital that has been accumulated during the first half of the year by the farmer is invested in seed, fertilizer, and capital improvements. Therefore, the potential for collection is greatly diminished. Third, improved targeting of VC Finance and Economy cadre reduced slightly the numbers of professional personnel available to extort sums of money.

b. Increased prices and rates. The dominant commodity produced in the Delta is rice, thus a change in the price and rate are both significant indications of VC intentions regarding extortion. The price of paddy for one gia increased from 800$VN in the second quarter to 1,000$VN during the third quarter. There are indications the price will go to 1,200$VN during the fourth quarter. Therefore, the amount of extortion can possibly show a rise even though numbers of collections are actually less. The rate of extortion is a more important indicator of VC intentions than the price because the rate is based on a constant unit of measurement - the "gia". Thus the discovery of a new rice table in Ba Xuyen Province, containing a general 5% rate increase, indicates the response to pressures and strains within the VC apparatus to use all available means to collect more funds during the third and fourth quarters of

F-1

CONFIDENTIAL

1972. While a 5% rise does not indicate desperation, it does show concern for obtaining additional collections. Prices on other commodities, businesses, and transportation also rose significantly. Part of these increases were due to inflation, but part of these were also due to VC efforts to improve total collections.

c. **Propaganda changes.** The changes in propaganda themes for the third quarter of 1972, reflected a desire to present a scenario of a winning VC/NVA drive into South Vietnam. According to a PRT report, a survey conducted in Vinh Long revealed that prior to the offensive, the VC propaganda theme was that the Liberation Forces are trying to drive out the Imperialist Americans, and everyone should want to contribute to the soldiers who are fighting the people's battles. Since the offensive, the theme has been that the people should pay tax to help provide the Front with foodstuffs to defend these provinces and save the people from American oppression. In the survey, a 70 year old respondent stated that when the VC came to collect from his family, they said the money would be sent to Quang Tri Province to rebuild houses for the people there. 29 respondents reported that the VC propaganda theme has changed to "The Liberation Front is going to take over some provinces in Western South Vietnam; people must pay tax to pay for foodstuffs for the VC forces." A 92 year old female respondent stated, "On 10 September 1972, the VC collected from me 7,000$VN tax and said that they just took over My Tho. This money will be used to support the soldiers so that they can have sufficient foodstuffs to defend My Tho." Although this bit of propaganda was obviously exaggerated since the VC did not occupy My Tho, it was used in an extortion effort. It is interesting to speculate that such pieces of propaganda may also reveal future intentions. These themes usually point out the official party line which the low ranking cadre are told to employ while extracting sums of money. In another survey conducted in Kien Phong, it was noted by several respondents that while the themes have not changed, "Since the last quarter of 1972, the VC shouted openly that they have won victories and victories. Especially, the US withdrawal was seen by the VC as an allied defeat." Another study in An Xuyen shows that the VC have been using revised themes both for taxation purposes and for youth enlistment in a manpower drive simultaneously being conducted. Two respondents to a PRT survey stated, "The VC usually lied and exaggerated their military victories, they spread rumors that the ARVN and Americans were defeated in all combat and they called the people to actively contribute manpower (enlist in the VC Army) and taxes to support the VC soldiers in the battlefields, prepare to open (the) 'Winter-Spring Campaign', and (to foment a) 'General Uprising' in the near future." It can be seen from these results of PRT surveys that the VC continue to mix fact with fiction to exaggerate their exploits, that the VC are preparing to occupy portions of MR4 during a ceasefire, and that they plan to foment a general uprising in the near future. To accomplish these aims, extortion remains their number one priority.

F-2

CONFIDENTIAL

1601 - 03 (S)

MEMORANDUM FOR: Senio Affair Advisor

SUBJECT: VC Taxation

1. The CG. has directed MACCORDS for action to develop a program to counter the VC taxation efforts.

2. At TAB A is a translation of a draft of the plan that the Deputy for POLWAR developed.

3. The Deputy for POLWAR will meet with Mr. Wilson 0830 hours, Wednesday, 20 September 1972, to discuss the anti-VC taxation problem.

4. At TAB B are some comments developed on the POLWAR plan.

5. Request you review the POLWAR plan and be prepared to brief Mr. Wilson on your recommendations concerning the plan. Your comments on the memorandum to POLWAR Advisor are encouraged.

Incl
  TAB A - Translation
  TAB B - Comments

JOHN C. ROGERS JR.
COL,   INF
MILITARY SENIOR ADVISOR

POLWAR PLAN TO PROPAGANDA AND CALL THE PEOPLE
TO ANTI THE COMMUNISTS TAXES PROGRAM

1.- DETERMINATION :

   After the US Air-strike to a number of importance strategy objectives in
the North(Hai Phong Ports Power plan, Ham Rong Bridge, etc...) therefore the
North VN now faced to a big difficulty on Economic and finance. In addition
the supply route from RUSSIA and CHINA to North VN and from North VN to South
VN all these supply route were under heavy strike by B-52. in this case the NVA
in the south VN received supply very little and very difficulty.
   In the RVN, especilly in the MR4, in 1971 and the first half of 1972, our
forces launched many operations, the NVA suffered heavy lost, many rear bases
and supply routes in cambodia and MR4 territorial were destroyed or heavily
damaged. Meanwhile our Pacification and development program are in good results
the communists' influence in the rural area are disapearing . In this case
the enemy become more disconcert day by day.
   In the last step, they are fighting with supply and
isolated, the Communists are trying to encourage people to stand up and to anti
the P&D program, in order to reocuppy the rural area and launch the taxes program
esppecially during the havest season they will rob rice from people to feed their
troop to prolong this war.
   Therefore, in the coming period the POLWAR have to disable the communists'
taxes program , and gain people to our side, this plan x have to launch in the
same time and all over MR4.

2.- MISSION:

   - To prevent and disable the communists taxes program.
   - Guide and encourage people to announce to GVN the communists' Economic &
     Finance cadres.
   - Division the communists's Economic & Finance (E&F) organization

3.- EXECUTION :

   a. Concept :
      (1) appeal to all level of people to anti comminists taxes program and
          the punishments to who paid taxes to communists.
      (2) Want to have people paticipate in our anti communists taxes program,
          our cadres must explain to people the advantage of announcing the
          communists E&F cadres to GVN, by doing that their life and property
          will be protected and their ID will be kept secret.
      (3) To division the communists E&F organization we appeal them to rally
          any E&F cadre rallied will be rewarded deservedly.
      (4) Creat the true and false rumor to people between communists E&F cadres
          and the communists who collect taxes and put on their pocket and sent
          our cadres to make up as comminists cadres to collect taxes and arrest
          anyone pay taxes or supply to communists.

                                                                  .-2

202

2 2

(5) give big reward to encourage people participate on parsuing the communists
E&F cadres.

b. FORM OF ACTIVITI ES:

Use all means of POLWAR, and information to propaganda in the following forms
(1) Appeal to people not to pay taxes ether money or rice to communists
if who paid taxes to communists will be must punished .
(2) Appeal to people to boycott the communists contribution.
(3) guide people to explain to communists why they can not pay taxes.
(4) Encourage people bring their rices to security area to store to prevent
communists to collect their rices.
(5) To prevent and anti communists propaganda we should organize x people
intelligent teams to collect informations on the rice mill, stores,
movie house, bus, villages and hamlets......
(6) Appeal to people announce the VCI to Phung Hoang commitee especially
the communists E&F cadres they will be rewarded.
(7) Appeal to communists E&F cadres to rally and they will be rewarded
deservedly.
(8) Appeal to people to imform to security agency if they received letter
or anyone come to collet taxes.
(9) Appeal to people to buycott the communists's public treasury certificate

c. Propaganda theme and subject (see inclose 1&2)

d. Period

1 Phase : from the date issue this plan to 31 Dec 72.
2 "   Will continus from Jan 73 to 30 Jun 73
3 "   Will be continue from 1 July 73 to 31 Dec 73.

e. MISSION TO EACH SECTION :

(a) MR4 Psywar office:
-Print assorted posters, slogans, leaflets, to support this plan.
-Print propaganda materials to support sector (when received request)
- follow up, supervide, to this plan.
(b) MR4 Indoctrination Section :
- Prepare study documents organize course to troop let them hnow the
anti communists taxes program, when on operation the troop will explain
and face to face communication to people.
- follow up units study course
(c) MR4 PRESS, RADIO, AND TV PROGRAM :
Base on the subject and theme inclosed to explain thru news paper, radio,
TV, program
- announce the result of this plan.
(d) THE 40th POLWAR BN:
organize show thru radio, TV program to anti propaganda anti communists
taxes program.
- use loudspeaker to broadcast explain the above plan.
- Print propaganda materials to support sector (when requested)

../ 3

203

3

(2) DIVISION AND SZ :
Use the Polwar Co assigned from 40th Polwar Bn to broadcast on operation area explain to people the anti communists taxes program, theme and subject are inclosed.
(3) SECTOR/POLWAR Co :
Increase the loudspeaker broudcast km (fix and mobile) to Villages, Hamlets, appeal to people not to pay taxes to communists, and who support or paid taxes to communists will be punsihed as current law discribed.
Increase the people intelligent teams to collect information and enemy propaganda.
Print poster, shogans, leaflets, appeal to people not to pay taxes to communists. put up at public area, and show slide on local movie house.
Organize study course to all Military, Gxxxx government employee and civilians to undertand the communists's taxes program, and how to prevent and help the prople to protect their rices.
Local news paper, radio program must announce on time all results of the operation especially disable or destroyed the communists's E&F organization or supply routes, in order to call the communists E&F cadres to rally.

4.- ADMIN & LOGISTIC :
    a. Support of leaflets and documents:
    - MR4 POLWAR BLOC
    - PSYWAR DEPARTMENT (if requested from MR4 POLWAR BLOC)
    b. Air Mission support:
    - 4th Air Division
    - Psywar Deparment (if requested from MR4 Polwar Bloc)

5.- COMMAND AND SIGNAL :
    a. Command:
    - POLWAR BLOC MR4
    b. Signal :
    - Use current signal system.
    - Report must sent to MR4 Polwar Bloc.

SLOGANS
—

to support the prevention of communists taxes program

1- The E&F cadres still exist, people' property will be rob   for

2- not pay tax to communists, because rice, and money are living needed for us

3- People must determind not to pay tax to communists.

4- Guide the National Police to arrest the communists E&F Cadres you will be rewarded.

5- The communists determined to make people become poorer and poorer

6- People should boycott all communists's contribution or collet taxes.

7- Pay taxes to the communists you will be punished by law.

8.-You should bring your rices to store in security afea to avoid communists to collect taxes or borrow your rice.

9- Announce VCI to local authority or ARVN unit to arrest them.

10- You must anounce to National Police when you received letter from communists ask you to pay taxes.

11- The Communists E&F cadres rally will be rewarded, if they bring along documents or mommunists money.

12- Announce to National Police of all E&F organization, your ID will be kept secret.

13- The Communists' public treasury certificate if a form of robbing your property.

PROPAGANDA THEME AND SUBJECT APPEAL TO PEOPLE TO
ANTI COMMUNISTS' TAXES PROGRAM

smsmsmsmsmsmsmsmsmsmsmsmsmsmsmsmsmsmsmsmsm smsmsmsmsmsmsmsmsmnemsmsmsmsmsmsmsmsm.smsmsmsmsmsmsmsmsmsmsmsm

Theme	Purport
1. Not pay tax to the communists	- The Communists in the NVN are under heavy air strike, the supply route were cut, Hai Phong Port was mined, they can not receive any supply from foreign country. - In the same time the NVA in SVN are heavily lost, all the supplies routes were cut, reveal from ralliers and POW's depositions now the communists are short of food, and money, to save the situation, the Communists are increasing collect of taxes to feed their troops, in order to prolong this war. - All kinds of taxes are not reasonable, all the taxes are set up by the Communists cadres in the local area, they forces people pay taxes as bus, lambretta, trucks, store, movie house, farmers... if anyone paid taxes to them one time then they will come back again to ask other kind of taxes, if people have no more money or rices to pay for them then they will announce that you against SLF. but in the same time if the GVN find out that people who paid taxes to communists then will be put in jail. - People should not pay taxes to communists cadres, when they are too hungry then they will rally to the GVN, the war will concluded sooner.
2. how to avoid to pay taxes to the communists.	- What shall you do, when the communists cadres come to collect taxes ? - People should say, if we pay taxes to you, when the GVN find out we will be put in jail, meanwhile we are very poor do not have enought rice to eat how can we pay taxes. can you come back next time. - a better way is that, tell the communists cadres come back tomorrow you will pay taxes for them, but when they leave, you should inform the National Police, (your ID will be kept secret) The National Police will make a plan to capture that communists cadre when thay come back to collect taxes, once the communists cadre were arrested no one will come to collect your taxes again, and you will be rewarded by GVN.
3. When you received a letter ask you to pay taxes what shall you do ?	- When you received a letter from the communists to ask you to pay taxes you should secretly inform the National Police, The National Police wil make a plan to arrest the cadres come to collect taxes from you, your life and property will be save and do not waste your money, to give to the communists.
4. the communists' public treasury certificate is it value at all ?	- The Communists public treasury certificate are not value at all, it is only a piece of paper, the communists use it to rob the people's properties. All people should boycott the communists public treasury certifi-cate.

206

5. if communists E&F cadres want to rally, what should they do

- The communists E&F cadres or cadres in the E&F organization want to rally, if follow these directives will be rewarded deservedly :
  * bring along taxes collect lists or documents
  * Bring along money collected from E&F organization.
  * find the collect taxes system from higher level to lower level
  * find out collect taxes system if havee documents for evidence will be better.

6. If you want to living in peaceful what shall you do

- No matter anywhere if the communists operatedin that area, the people will have to sufferedsorrowful and mourning.
- If the communists operate in your area you will never can living in peacefull because the communists, they want the people become poorer and poorer then the people will listen to communists to struggle and againt the GVN.
- Therefore if you want to living in peace you must announce to Phung Hoang Committee or National Police, local authority, or ARVN to arrest those VCI or communists cadres, located in your area.

7. Rumour

- launch rumour to make people disbeleived and do not know who are communists E&F cadres or people come to make money or GVN's cadres make up as communists cadres come to collect taxes, then if you pay taxes you will be put in jail. by doing so the people will afraid to pay taxes to the communists.